Blessing in
mosque and mission

Blessing in mosque and mission

Larry G. Lenning

William Carey Library

1705 N. SIERRA BONITA AVE. • PASADENA, CALIFORNIA 91104

Library of Congress Cataloging in Publication Data

Lenning, Larry G.   1939–
   Blessing in Mosque and Mission.

   Bibliography: p.
   Includes indexes.
   1. Missions to Muslims   2. Blessing and cursing.
3. Barakah. I. Title.
BV2625.L38   261.2'7   80-25110
ISBN 0-87808-433-9

Published by the William Carey Library
P.O. Box 128-C
Pasadena, California 91104
Telephone (213) 798-0819

In accord with some of the most recent thinking of the aca-
demic press, the William Carey Library is pleased to present
this scholarly book which has been prepared from an author-
edited and author-prepared camera ready copy.

PRINTED IN THE UNITED STATES OF AMERICA

To
LEE
whose love I cherish

and to
Tim
Bob
Kristi
*the four people
who have brought
to me the greatest
blessings a man could
ever ask for in his life*

Contents

Foreword

I am one of those fortunate people who lived in West Africa
during the years when the Church was awakening to Islam. In
the early 1950's it was most unlikely that anyone would have
worked through a concept which assumes commonality between
Christianity and Islam. West Africa was still in the grip
of a special kind of history which had cast the two religions
as adversaries. The antiquity of Islam, reaching back to the
14th century, even earlier in the regions of Chad and Bornu,
made Christianity, by comparison, a recent religion. The
pragmatic way that both England and France used Fulani emirs
in the rule of their colonies is well known. Resentment by
pagan peoples to Muslim power was intense. Coupled with
these factors was the idea that to be truly African was to be
Muslim, since nations now on the brink of independence saw
Christianity as a system which came along with colonialism.
This was not a false claim in many ways. Islam had interacted
with African traditional life and culture over so many years,
that even the remotest traditional villages revealed an Islamic bias through innuendos of language and unconscious ha-
bits of life.

I was the principal and only teacher in a catechist's
training school in Northern Nigeria in those days--more than
twenty years ago. The resentment which Christian leaders had
toward Muslims was concentrated in their ideas of Christian
witness. A natural talent for hostile argument with Muslims,
at every turn, had obviously been augmented by the teaching
of missionaries who, likewise, saw Islam as the adversary.
The greatest problems with which I had to deal arose not only

from the socio-political bias in which Christians found themselves, but from honest convictions which Christian leaders
had; Muslims had corrupted the Bible, ridiculed the death of
Christ, and were generally leading immoral lives. I shall
not forget the encounters my students had with Muslims on
weekends, when they left the school for ministering in nearby
villages. Their exchanges with Muslims were reported back in
great detail. The arguments, loud and bitter, had little
light and scarcely any love.

But the mood changed during the decade of the 60's. In
spite of tensions following independence, which often involved Muslims in politics, serious study of Islam by Christian leaders began with high interest. The Islam in Africa
Project brought help which was needed soon after 1960. Members of the IAP teams not only conducted seminars lasting
several days in various centers, but visited churches and
conferences, speaking in positive ways about African Islam
and encouraging study of the Qur'an and Muslim history. This
new spirit of understanding resulted in more favorable contact with Muslims. Missions, as well as their churches,
caught the spirit of reasonable attitudes towards and creative interaction with Muslims.

To focus on areas of continuity between Islamic and
Christian belief and practice, is the approach which fosters
openness and understanding. The spirit which Larry Lenning
brings to his study on the concept of *baraka* is important,
for it models an attitude of mutuality rather than controversy. It is not meant to say that "blessing" has identical
expression or meaning in both traditions. However, where
human needs are being met through something as prominent in
thought and practice as *baraka*, and where areas of agreement
are so convincing in both religions, we must take seriously
the commonality of the two faiths and the fact that believers
can address each other with respect and understanding. The
willingness to take the continuity between religions seriously, not only makes Christians more aware of the areas of
truth shared with Islam, but also sharpens the distinctives
and differences between the faiths. The result is a clarifi-
cation of one's own faith and a more objective understanding
of the faith of another.

One may feel uncomfortable with an approach to Muslims
through the concept of *baraka*, because it is connected so
closely with folk Islam and animistic structures. *Baraka*
in the Muslim world. and West Africa in particular, is in
close alliance with traditional practices. It carries a tacit

approval of rites and charms which are out of harmony with a liberating Gospel. While this is granted, still Christians must remember that the lineage of our own faith is out of the Hebrew tradition where symbols and rituals, even objects, carried tremendous power for good to individuals and the community. Christianity embraces the highest teachings as to what "blessing" means in terms of God's grace and love. Nevertheless, within this same Christianity, taken worldwide, may be found practices which are very little different from the "blessing" promised by a Fulani cleric to his followers in Northern Cameroon. This kind of study keeps us from too much idealism about our own faith. Humility, after all, is a virtue which Christians still need very much. It is a great help in relating to followers of another faith.

The comprehensive and sensitive way that Dr. Lenning has handled this subject gives us not only a model for attitude, but also for reaching into the deepest areas of two faiths, as we are faithful in our Christian witness to the Muslim world. We are able to see, again, how much can be shared and learned, and how Christians and Muslims are brought closer together in the process.

> Dean S. Gilliland
> Assistant Professor of Con-
> textualized Theology and
> African Studies
> Fuller Theological Seminary
> Pasadena, California

Preface

Tremendous potential exists for the Christian Church as it considers incorporating the dynamic concept of blessing into its ministry, worship, outreach, and theology. In encountering Islam and traditional African religions which have deep roots in this vast continent, the Church must necessarily work to bridge the gaps that have developed. Blessing can become a key link as its potential is discovered and used to make the Gospel of Christ valid and meaningful for these children of God. The author is convinced, based on his experience in Cameroon and on his studies, that the concept of blessing can make the adventure of mission a fruitful one in Islamic Africa, particularly in West Africa.

I am grateful for the guidance received at Fuller Theological Seminary, Pasadena, California, in the development of this book which is a revision of my doctoral dissertation. I especially want to thank Dean S. Gilliland, Arthur F. Glasser, and Charles H. Kraft. Special thanks are also due Dr. Ken Wagner and Dr. and Mrs. Oscar T. Lenning who read the manuscript and offered constructive criticisms and suggestions. I also owe a debt of gratitude to the Division of World Missions and Inter-Church Cooperation of the American Lutheran Church, its missionaries working with me in Cameroon, and to the African pastors, evangelists, and catechists who brought to me keener insight and perspective on the potential of blessing in the life of the Church. Appreciation is extended to Dr. Roland Miller, Editor of the Series on Islamic Studies for his positive review of the original manuscript and for his precise and helpful suggestions.

The insights and perspectives offered in this book are
hopefully only the beginning of further exploration and
study by Church leaders and Muslim leaders throughout the
world where Christians and Muslims encounter each other.
The author is admittedly a Christian, but he trusts that he
has been fair in his study of Islam and the Qur'an and that
no unfair bias and no bigotry is discovered. He hopes that
the power of blessing can be used and adapted throughout both
the Muslim and Christian worlds by the Church as it attempts
to make its faith in the One, True God more alive and vital.

Finally, I am most gracious to my lovely wife Lee whose
patience and love were constant incentives to complete the
writing and publishing of this book. Her help with the proof-
reading of the manuscript has left a book with few typograph-
ical errors.

Larry G. Lenning
Granada Hills,
California

I

Introduction

Because of events in the Middle East in the beginning of the
1980's, the concern for and reaction to Muslims has greatly
heightened. Many western Christians are puzzled by Islam,
its leaders, and its view of life. We saw an aging leader,
Ayatollah Khomeini, sitting atop his home in the sacred city
of Qom, and we wondered how he could demand such devout
discipleship and obedience. What did he possess that led
countless people to demonstrate daily, to retain hostages
for a long period of time, to pray with increased fervor and
devotion? The answer, in great part, is that he was viewed
as a man who exuded the power of blessing and charisma, a
holy man who demanded great respect and honor.

There have been other such great religious leaders.
Abraham of Ur, father of the Israelis and Arabs alike, was
a man of great blessing. The power of blessing he received
from God became highly treasured and sought after. Jesus of
Nazareth also was a blessed man, bringing hope, new life,
and salvation to those who believed and followed him.

Does the fact that these three men share the power of
blessing mean anything to us? What does it say about
increasing the effectiveness of Christian communication and
witness of the Gospel to Muslims?

This book explores the biblical and Islamic understanding
of blessing with the aim of discovering its potential for
creating deeper ties between Islam and Christianity. Our
study attempts to focus on Christian-Muslim relationships in
an African context, particularly West Africa.

1

Blessing in Christian
Mission to Muslims in Africa

Christians believe that God is at work in the world; that
the world which he created is the world which he is in the
process of redeeming and renewing. It is a pluralistic
world with people struggling in a continuing search for
justice, peace, and abundant, eternal life. Within this
pluralism Christians encounter several major religions. One
significant religious force in the world today is Islam.
Christians and Muslims find themselves living together as
neighbors, as fellow human beings. They encounter each
other both at the market place and at top governmental
levels. They often are observants at each other's religious
festivals.

Most Christians and Muslims understand their faith as
giving them a mission. Their understanding of mission has
often led to confrontation and enmity. The result has been
conquest, occupation, and increasing tension between com-
peting societies. In some countries where one religion is
dominant, the other religion is banned as a threat to
society. Political tensions have too often led to the
undermining of any move toward openness and cooperation.

Fortunately, there has grown in many parts of the world,
especially within the last decade, a new openness and
willingness to share and communicate with one another.
Correspondingly, several Muslim communities have become
increasingly open to listen to the Gospel.

The degree of the Church's effectiveness in communicating both a spirit of openness to the Muslim world and, at the same time, being true to its calling of discipling the nations of the world, is often dependent on its methodology and approach. Often the witness of the Church has been weak because it has tied its message too much to one particular culture or world view.

This book is an attempt to focus on one concept that may help the Christian Church increase its effectiveness in its witness to the Muslim world. The primary aim will be to enhance the positive impact of the Gospel on the Muslim communities of West Africa. However, the insights gained through this study will, hopefully, be applicable to mission outreach in Muslim communities in other parts of the world as well.

BACKGROUND FOR THE STUDY

There are two primary reasons why this book is being written. One is that the Church is called by Christ to bring the Gospel to all people, including Muslims. The second is that there have been some serious problems that have hindered the Church's witness to Muslims.

Our Call To Witness To The Muslim World

When Jesus commanded his followers to make disciples of all nations, he set in motion the world of Christian mission. Empowered by the Holy Spirit, the early Christians spread out through the eastern Mediterranean area, proclaiming the good news of salvation and eternal life in Jesus Christ. Their response of witnessing and establishing churches was understood by them as fulfilling their call to be faithful to Jesus' command.

This call to witness has continued to be a basic driving force throughout the history of the Church down to the present. A vital aspect of the Church's call to witness today clearly includes the over 700 million Muslims in the world.

Primary Factors Affecting The Church's Witness to Muslims

The task of witnessing to Muslims, of bringing them into a faith relationship with God as He revealed himself in Jesus Christ, has been and continues to be a difficult one. There are several reasons why this is so.

A historically negative attitude. A major aspect of this overall difficulty is that the Christian Church has historically had a negative attitude toward Islam. Ever since Islam began in the deserts of southwest Arabia, the Church has been in a position of reaction with this competitive new faith. No sooner had the orphan/trader Muhammad become founder and leader of a new monotheistic religion, than the Christian community reacted to this challenge on the horizon. Both Jews and Christians alike felt the threat of Islam as Muslims began their expansion.

It did not take long for Muslim warriors to conquer the Middle East and the northern coast of Africa. The Christian Church in these areas, wracked by division and other weakening forces, quickly fell prey to the effective onslaughts of this new religion. Only the militaristic defenses of Charles Martel and his soldiers prevented Islam from conquering all of Europe.

Historians have painted tragic pictures of the fate of Christians who stood fast against the Islamic advance. The Church lost both lives and converts to Islam. The Church, naturally, became defensive and antagonistic. The Muslim conquest was, no doubt, a major disaster for the Church in the 8th to 15th centuries. The Church lost all vestiges of prestige and a dominant position in mid-eastern governments. "The Muslim sense of superiority naturally found itself reflected in a Christian sense of inferiority" (Neill, 1964: 64).

As the Christian Church entered its second millenium it took a more offensive stance toward Muslims. Hatred toward them deepened. Christians saw Muslims as unbelievers who had no right to live, especially in the Holy Land. One could slaughter them without pity or guilt because one was doing it to the glory of God. Thus the Church embarked on the crusades against the Arabs. However, these attempts to win back the holy shrines of Palestine from the Muslims resulted in death and destruction for Christians and Muslims alike. These voyages to the east left trails of anger and bitterness that remain in the hearts and minds of many Christians and Muslims even today.

Throughout this period very little, if any, effort was made to convert Muslims to Christ. In some areas Muslims were tolerated to the extent that they could practice their faith in freedom. But, in general, the hope and aim of the Church was the extinction of Islam.

In the 15th to 18th centuries Muslims were seen by the
Church as a menace in eastern Europe. In the forward surge
of the Ottoman Turks, many Christians became Muslims, and
again, in the eyes of the Church, Islam was the ugly adversary. Martin Luther and other reformers were prevented from
developing a far-reaching theology of mission for several
reasons, one of which was the Islamic threat marauding its
way from Turkey into the Balkans. This lack of a theology
of mission did not mean that Luther and the other reformers
were totally ignorant of Islam. For example, Luther was
ahead of his time in asking that the Church seriously study
Islam and its tenets. As early as 1519 in his discussion
of Psalm 2 he wrote that the Muslim Turks "ought to be
conquered by increasing the number of Christians among them"
(Pelikan, 1958:334). In his sermon against the Turks in
1529 (*Heerpredigt wider den Türken*) Luther suggests that the
Christians who had been captured by the Muslims had a missionary responsibility (Luther, 1964:194-95).

Calls for mission to Muslims, such as those made by
Luther, had little impact on the Protestant community. It
was not until the 19th century that the Church began to take
seriously its task of discipling the nations, which included
all Muslims. The usual attitude at the time in the hearts
and minds of the missionaries to Muslims was to convert them
to the Christian faith, to remove them from the "dregs" of
Islam, and bring them to the Light of the world. The negative attitude that had become engrained in Christianity
toward Muslims continued to affect the Christian missionary
adversely in his work among Islamic people. Even though
hate began to be replaced by love and respect, there was
still a deep feeling in the lives of many Christian missionaries that Muslims needed to be rescued from the "hellish
depths" of Islamic philosophies, cultures, and beliefs.
Therefore many went as conquerors of Islam. With such
attitudes they seldom took time to study and understand the
Muslim world. They had little empathy for the ways a Muslim
practiced his faith in Allah. Even the word "Allah" was
seen by some as the name of another false god.

A current dichotomous approach. It was in the 20th
century that some Christians began to have second thoughts
about their approaches to Muslims. As they interacted
with Muslims, they discovered that their attitudes had
been tainted with prejudice and conceit. They began to
rediscover many of the things Christians and Muslims have in
common. They discovered common attitudes toward Old Testament leaders. To the amazement of many they discovered
that the Qur'an praises Jesus a great deal.

This rediscovery led to two different reactions. On the one hand, some theologians within the Christian Church who had studied Islam thought the proper solution was to view Islam and Christianity as different but equally valid paths leading toward the same goal. According to this view, described by Kraemer (1962), Islam and Christianity are "expressions of the same truth, apprehended and construed in different ways" (p. 57).

Conversely, there were Christians who accepted this joint Christian-Muslim heritage, but who firmly believed that Jesus Christ is the only way, truth, and life. They were prepared to come to Muslims, not as conquerors ready to extract the Muslim from his community, but as brothers with a message of love, hope, faith, and abundant life. These ambassadors of Christ started with a positive note, emphasizing the many things Muslims and Christians have in common: faith in the one true God, a common inheritance from Abraham, a positive view toward the significant roles of Moses, David, and other prophets, and a common exalting view of Jesus of Nazareth.

Such missionaries came not only with positive, common theologies, but also with common anthropologies. Both Christians and Muslims are sinful, needing divine grace. Both are living in a world of meaningful ritual, myth, and family relationships. Both are deeply conscious of the limitations of man and his need for reconciliation. Both see the societal dimensions of life as being significant.

This dichotomy of approaches has caused many periods of inner hardship for the Church as it struggles with the task of bringing Christ to Muslims. The Church has struggled continuously with its often ethnocentric approaches to Islam. It has wanted to allow the Muslim to retain his cultural heritage, yet has wondered if a Muslim could really become a Christian without adopting at least some accepted "western" features of the Christian faith.

A western-dominated world view. A corresponding aspect of this multi-faceted problem is the fact that the Christian Church, by and large, has developed its hermeneutic and methodology in the last two centuries out of a predominantly western "scientific" world view. Such an upbringing creates problems for the missionary when he encounters such aspects of Islam as determinism, mysticism, devotion to saints, pilgrimages, and the wearing of amulets for protection. A science-oriented messenger of the Gospel is frustrated when

he encounters a non-linear concept of time, little or no
concern for progress and development, and everything else
that comes as a consequence of a theology that is strongly
fatalistic and non-scientific in scope.

This western-dominated world view causes problems not
only for the Christian missionary. The non-western receiver
of the Gospel often feels that the message as proclaimed
does not fit his view of reality. Because the message has
been shaped by a foreign culture, he often does not see it
as a valid option for him to consider within his own culture.
He sometimes tends to equate the messenger of the Gospel
with a western political or economic representative. The
result is that he rejects the Gospel because he is unable to
separate the message from the messenger and the forms and
methods in which this message is proclaimed.

DESCRIPTION OF THE STUDY

In spite of many problems and difficulties, the Church
continues today to grapple with its call to witness to the
Muslim community. It is working hard to build bridges over
which Christians and Muslims can communicate and share their
respective faiths.

Both ecumenical and evangelical churches and mission
societies have become increasingly conscious of their responsibility to witness to Muslims. In the past decade, the
World Council of Churches has sponsored a series of dia-
logues to which Christian and Muslim religious leaders have
been invited. In these encounters the participants have
tackled subjects ranging from revelation and shared community to mission and *da'wah* (the invitation or call to conversion).

In the 1970's, two conferences were convened by evangelicals to discuss the Church's mission to Muslims. In Jan-
uary of 1976, the Commission of the Approach to those of
Non-Christian Faiths of the Evangelical Alliance sponsored
such a gathering at High Wycombe, England. The participants
combined intellectual Christian reflection on the Muslim
world with a renewed empathy for Muslims. "What appeared to
be refreshingly new was their unique perspective on dialogue
with Muslims" (Glasser, 1976:260). (The July 1976 issue of
Missiology contains several papers presented at this conference.)

In October 1978, the North American Conference on Muslim Evangelization was held at Colorado Springs, Colorado. A result of the Lausanne Congress on Evangelism, the conference had for a goal the development of a fairly comprehensive strategy for Muslim evangelization. The interactions and discussions held were based on the insights of approximately forty papers written and read prior to the conference. (A compendium containing these papers and a variety of responses are published in *The Gospel and Islam: A 1978 Compendium*, edited by Don M. McCurry.) The establishment of the Samuel Zwemer Institute in Pasadena, California is a direct consequence of this conference. This multi-purpose center is designed to be a teaching-training institute that will do research in Islam and promote the cause of missions to Muslims.

The concern of the Church and these conferences is to build bridges to Islam. One concept that is potentially helpful in building effective bridges to Islam is that of blessing. This concept is discussed here along with an outline of how this study will attempt to integrate it into an effective approach of witnessing to Muslims.

The Concept Underlying This Study

The concept of blessing will undoubtedly appeal to many people concerned with mission to Muslims. There is clear evidence of its centrality in the biblical record as well as in Islamic contexts. One also finds it a valid concept in the general study of religion.

Defining the concept. Blessing is a concept that is basic to Jewish, Christian, and Muslim thought. The most common definition of blessing is "divine favor" or "benediction." However, a more complete definition must include the ideas of beneficient force, efficient power, the holy or holiness, the sacred, and charisma.

In the English language, "blessing" has tended to lose much of its dynamics and has become rather shallow in meaning and impact. Unfortunately, it has often been reduced to formulas people use to pray before eating or to express concern for one who has sneezed. Even in the Church, the word "blessing" often has the connotation of simply signifying the end of the worship service.

This is in stark contrast to the dynamic power of blessing found in the Scriptures. For the Old Testament people

of God, blessing was a vital force which is a gift of God
and which saturates the soul. It was an inner power, a
vital power, a power of holiness, related closely to prosperity and wisdom (Pedersen, 1926:167). The Hebrews believed that blessing gave one the ability to live life to its
fullest and deepest sense. Believing that God gave blessing, they saw it as a holy power which controlled their
lives.

The dynamic impact of blessing continues in the New
Testament where it is proclaimed by Jesus and the apostles
as a spiritual power with eternal ramifications. Blessing
is viewed as a corollary of salvation because of its holistic, ongoing, regular role in God's relationship with the
Church.

Blessing is also a vital concept in Islam. While its
meaning in classical Islam is often quite different from
that of "popular" Islam, its validity as a potent force
is widely recognized.

In *A Dictionary of Non-Christian Religions*, Parrinder
(1973) describes the Arabic word for blessing (*baraka*) as:

An Arabic word which means "blessing," and which is widely used throughout the Islamic world to denote a mysterious and wonderful power, a blessing from God, indicating
holiness or "blessed virtue." Baraka...is possessed by
saints, and the prophet Muhammad possessed it in the
highest degree.... Baraka is seen in miracles, holy
places and people, prayers, blessings, and curses (p. 40).

It is because Christians, Jews, and Muslims have a common
Semitic inheritance that all three share the concept of
blessing. The Hebrew word for blessing is *berakah* or *baruk*,
the stem being *brk*. The Greek words used in the New Testament are *eulogeo* and *makarizo*, but their content and meaning are greatly influenced by the Old Testament. As seen
already, the Arabic word for blessing is *baraka* (the stem is
also *brk*). Thus, we have a linguistic tie with Islam that
hopefully will serve us well as we attempt to build bridges
to our Muslim friends over which they may come to a living
faith relationship with Jesus Christ.

Validity of the concept in the study of religion. In
addition to being a basic concept in Islam and in biblical
literature, blessing is a vital and valid concept within the
general study of religion and religious experience. The
study of religion by sociologists and psychologists indi-

cates that the concept of blessing, the sacred, the holy, charisma, is a basic phenomenon in man's religious life.

Emile Durkheim, in studying man and his human experience, concluded that all of man's experiences can be classified into two opposite categories, namely the sacred and the profane. In his book *The Elementary Forms of the Religious Life*, Durkheim (1954) described the profane as man's normal, ongoing, routine experiences in life. The profane could be predicted; it was caused by man's own actions, reflections, and decisions. The sacred, on the other hand, comes into man's life and existence from outside himself. It is unpredictable; it is powerful and mysterious. It elicits within man a response of awe and wonder which leads further to worship and observance of and participation in ritual. In experiencing the sacred, attitudes and sets of practices are established.

While Durkheim gave this power, this force that comes from outside of man into his life, the name of "sacred," Rudolf Otto (1950) calls it the "holy." In his book *The Idea of the Holy*, Otto describes the "holy" as that which is at the innermost core of religion. It is a living force, filled with mystery. Otto believed that man can sense the holy in his feelings. Often the experience of the holy leads a believer to feel unworthy in its presence.

In commenting on Otto's thesis, Fallding (1974) says:

To be touched by the holy in this approach can be a ravishing, transporting, intoxicating experience. In the attitude of worship the drawing away and drawing near are wedded together. One enters worship to be touched by the beyond. Otto writes as a theologian centrally concerned with the holy as an object of direct experience. He does, of course, accept the reality of it. It is also very important that he treats it as a highly generalized object, available for approach through diverse systems of belief... Because of its being a real constraint and a real possibility for one's life it can be intimately felt (p. 40).

While Otto does not come out of a strong sociological orientation as does Durkheim, his description of the holy is remarkably similar to Durkheim's concept of the sacred. Both indicate that this concept is basic to man's religious experience.

A third scholar, Max Weber (1947) labels this concept "charisma." In his book *The Theory of Social and Economic Organization*, Weber defines charisma in the following way:

> A certain quality of an individual personality by virtue of which he is set free apart from ordinary men and treated as endowed with supernatural, superhuman, or at least specifically exceptional powers or qualities. These are such as are not accessible to the ordinary person, but are regarded as of divine origin or as exemplary, and on the basis of them the individual concerned is treated as a leader   (p. 358-59).

Weber focused major attention on the creativity and tremendous impulse that charisma gives through special people to society at large. For him charisma has a beckoning quality that attracts people who respond with deep conviction. Those special people who have a "charismatic mission" perform the extraordinary as opposed to the ordinary.

The Approach and Scope of the Study

Any study of a concept that is aimed at being useful in the life and mission of the Church should be developed from a certain perspective. From this perspective one attempts to approach the subject in an orderly, systematic, and objective manner so that its usefulness is assured and the desired goal for the study is attained. All possible sources of relevant evidence to which access is possible must be thoroughly explored.

The perspective and approach. Focusing, at least initially, on those aspects of Islam and Christianity that are similar can become one positive approach to encounter, dialogue, and conversion. It is from this perspective that this study on the concept of blessing is written. This is not to say that we are abandoning our faith in Jesus Christ as the "only name under heaven given to men by which we must be saved" (Acts 4:12). It does not mean that our hope that Muslims come to accept Jesus Christ as Lord and Savior is discarded or that basic differences are ignored. It does mean that the basic responsibility of conversion is that of the Holy Spirit. It also means that the step of preparation must necessarily precede the steps of presence, proclamation, and persuasion.

Understanding the concept of blessing is an important part of this initiatory step of preparation. It is impor-

tant so that we can come to the Muslim as a friend who has
received this common concept from God. This study is based
on the premise that discovering the holistic meaning and
role of blessing and its vital relationship to ritual and
faith can become one pillar of a necessary bridge that will
allow the Muslim to overcome theological barriers that
divide Muslims and Christians, and instead, establish and
build up in the Muslims' life a new faith-allegiance to God
in Jesus Christ.

Because the concept of blessing is such a fundamental and
widespread one in the annals of religious history, this book
is basically a survey of the concept. We will study the
impact it has had and can have in the history of God's people
throughout the Old and New Testaments and in the Church today. Because our aim is to increase the effectiveness of
the Church's mission in West Africa, we will discuss the
role of blessing in the Muslim world in general, and more
specifically in West Africa.

It is necessary at this point that the reader realize
that in the Islamic world the majority of Muslims are
adherents to what is called "popular" Islam, in contrast to
"ideal" or "classical" Islam. In popular Islam one finds
a radical awareness of and devotion to mystical, "animistic"
power. Such Muslims seek this power in a variety of objects
and people. Popular Islam is a mixture of Islamic and animistic practices and beliefs. In popular Islam the meanings
attached to the forms of religious expression are radically
different from classical Islam. "Popular" Muslims may be
aware of the theological intent and impact of blessing as
espoused in the Qur'an, but they often understand it in
terms of animistic categories. "Witchcraft, sorcery, spells,
and charms are the background of the native Muslim psychology
to an extent that is realized only by those who have pene-
trated most deeply into the life of the people" (Zwemer,
1939:Intro.).

While the concept of blessing described in this study is
not identical with the animistic *baraka* sought by many
"popular" Muslims, its characteristic as benevolent power
and holiness that comes from God will speak to these Muslims. Hopefully, a deeper understanding of blessing as
divine benediction bestowed by God will help adherents of
"popular" Islam come to a clearer grasp of God and his relationship with man through faith.

Because the "best learning takes place by discovery"
(Kraft, 1974:25), the author firmly believes that if "popular" Muslims of West Africa were to discover the total
meaning and impact of blessing, they would be better able
to divert their allegiance from animistic *baraka* to *baraka*
as holistic spiritual blessing that comes from God. Hopefully, in this way they would become more receptive to the
Gospel.

This book is written to show that a deeper understanding
of blessing as expounded in the Scriptures and in classical
Islam will enhance the reception of Christ as Lord and
Savior. It does not deny the need for power encounter to
take place within the receptor society. "The central
issue in God's confrontation of any man is his authority
and Christ's Lordship. This means 'power encounter'--for
the divine power that confronts and woos is inevitably re-
sisted by the human spirit" (Glasser, 1979:133). But when
the blessing of God is understood as a holistic power that
touches all areas of a believer's life, when West Africans
experience this power that is designed to affect both the
individual and the community, then many Muslims in this
region will become more receptive to the Good News. They
will be better able to shift their allegiance to Christ
while remaining within their own cultural milieu (Kraft,
1979:343).

Comprehending the dynamic impact of blessing can become
a double benevolence. Not only will Muslims in Africa become more receptive to the Gospel, but the Christian Church
throughout the world can deepen and enrich its understanding
of and appreciation for the comprehensive power of blessing
that is often lacking today. As the Church discovers the
impact that blessing had in the Old and New Testaments, it
will hopefully realize that this powerful concept has
tremendous potential for its own life and growth, and for
mission to both classical and "popular" Muslims.

This discovery has been the experience of the author. In
spite of the fact that, as a Lutheran, I was aware of the
concept of blessing, too often it was taken for granted as a
necessary but certainly not a vital part of the life of the
Church. Within the liturgy it played a minor role. Outside
the context of worship, blessing had little conscious impact on my life.

It was during my service as a missionary to Cameroon,
West Africa, that the power of blessing became more evident

and alive. As several African church leaders shared with me
their insights into the Bible, especially the Old Testament,
as I observed the far-ranging influence of the power of
blessing (*baraka*) in the lives of Muslims and non-Muslims
alike, my understanding of blessing as a holistic dynamic
force started to develop.

Because I was working in an area where "popular" Islam
was particularly strong, I struggled (and still struggle)
with the tension that exists in trying to distinguish
clearly between blessing as animistic *baraka* and blessing
as holistic spiritual *baraka* that has its source in God.

I began to incorporate blessing into my personal life
through the laying on of hands on our children each evening
prior to their going to sleep. This act alone created a
deeper awareness in my family of the presence and power of
God through blessing. The role of blessing within the arena
of worship took on new significance. I experienced a deeper
sensitivity to God's blessing within liturgical rituals,
greetings and benedictions, the proclaimed word, and in the
sacraments and other rites of the Church. This present
study has expanded my appreciation of and enthusiasm for the
dynamic role of blessing within the Church, especially in
its mission to the total life of Muslims in Africa.

For this study, information drawn from published mater-
ials was supplemented by my personal experience while living
in West Africa for five years. In addition, material was
obtained by interviewing West Africans who are studying
in the United States and missionaries who have worked in
West Africa.

This study is limited in certain respects. First of all,
I do not read Arabic. Therefore, it was impossible to go to
some of the original sources in Islamic literature. Very
little of the Arabic literature in this area has been
translated into the languages in which I am proficient
(English, French, German, and Fulani). Fortunately, several
of the major relevant works and others have been summarized
in secondary sources.

Secondly, some of the major West African works in this
area have been written in Hausa. Here several key works
have been translated into English.

A third limitation is that the location of several works
to which reference was found could not be identified or

obtained. The author is confident, however, that no major
sources fall into this category.

We shall, first of all in section two, focus on the fascinating world of Islam in general and Islamic Africa in
particular. We will begin with a discussion of the concept
of blessing in Islam and its impact on the life of Muhammad.
We shall discover that even though the word *baraka* is not
found very often in the Qur'an, it was and has become a dominant theme and force in Islam.

In Africa there are some areas where the concept of *baraka* is especially strong and significant, such as Morocco in
North Africa. We shall briefly study aspects of North
African Islam such as maraboutism and the veneration of
saints.

We shall also study the relevance of blessing in Islamic
West Africa. We shall investigate this power as it emanates
from the lives of learned men and Muslim teachers such as
Shehu Usman dan Fodio, a Fulani who became a powerful force
in the early years of the nineteenth century.

In section three we will probe the Bible to see what
impact blessing had in the lives of God's people since the
creation of the world. Not only will we discover that God
is the source and giver of blessing, but that without it
there would have been no covenant, no formation of a people
of God, no proper worship. In the life, death, and resurrection of Jesus we shall see the close relationship of
blessing to salvation. The New Testament gives us many
passages that show the powerful impact of the new aspects of
blessing on the life and mission of the Church, its worship
patterns, and how blessing was communicated to the people of
God.

Finally, in section four we shall describe how the concept of blessing as a comprehensive, holistic power should
and can become a key link in building a bridge to Islam.
It will be noted that too often the concept of blessing
has been neglected or rejected because of magical, superstitious interpretations or tie with animism that many
missionaries have given it. With the insights obtained from
previous chapters, which should give a solid, positive base
for the use of blessing in mission, we shall attempt to indicate some realistic, practical, affirming ways in which the
concept of blessing can be emphasized in the outreach and
life of the Church in West Africa.

Previous research.   As far as the author knows, no one
has written on the concept of blessing in the way this book
is being written.   This study is a biblical and Islamic survey of the concept which is followed by applying the insights
gained to help make the Church become a more effective witness and disciple-maker.   A number of scholars have dealt
with the concept in specific areas, with the most significant ones being discussed here.

Among those who have written on the subject of blessing
in the Old Testament, Johannes Pedersen, a Danish theologian
in the early 20th century, is perhaps the most significant.
In his book *Israel, Its Life and Culture* (1926, 1940), Pedersen gives the reader a phenomenological understanding of
blessing.   He focuses on the power of the spoken word and
sees blessing as an element of vitality.   He stresses especially the contrast between the naturalistic view of blessing as an impersonal, supernatural force and Israel's view
of blessing as a powerful gift of God and an expression of
his personality.

Sigmund Mowinckel, a Norwegian scholar, follows Pedersen's approach closely and studies the concept of blessing in its liturgical, cultic setting.   In *The Psalms in
Israel's Worship* (1962), he emphasizes the communal function
of blessing.

Another study of blessing is by Josef Scharbert.   In the
first book of a trilogy, *Solidarität in Segen und Fluch im
Alten Testament und in seiner Umwelt, I. Vaterfluch und
Vatersegen* (1958), he studies blessing and cursing and
their functions as elements which maintain the cohesiveness
of Israel's social life.   He highlights the important role
of the father as the mediator of blessing.

In the area of the New Testament, a major, but old, book
is by Lyder Brun: *Segen und Fluch im Urchristentum* (1932).
Brun accentuates the fact that God is the source of blessing and that Jesus in the New Testament becomes the mediator
in the transmission of blessing from God to man.

A more recent book is *Der Segen im Neuen Testament* (1967)
by Wolfgang Schenk.   He states that blessing signifies God's
redemptive activity in Christ, and is thus synonomous with
salvation.   As such it loses its distinctive meaning and
becomes only words of petition.

The most recent major work on blessing is by Claus Westermann. In his book *Blessing in the Bible and the Life of
the Church* (1978), he provides a necessary corrective to
Schenk. Westermann maintains that there is a close relationship between blessing and salvation, but he deems it
necessary and crucial to distinguish them from each other
and keep them in proper tension.

In the Arabic-speaking Islamic world we find sporadic
treatment of blessing. A fairly recent major article on
the subject is *"La Baraka chez les Arabes"* by Joseph Chelhod
(1955). In this article he distinguishes clearly between
blessing that has its source in God and animistic blessing.
In doing so he presents blessing as a major force in Islamic
society.

A major contribution to the subject from the perspective
of Morocco is given by Edvard Westermarck. Even though
three of his books deal with the concept of blessing, it is
his book *Ritual and Belief in Morocco* (1926) that goes into
great detail in explaining the powerful influence of *baraka*
in the lives of Muslims. He is especially helpful in describing the power of blessing as seen in the veneration of
saints.

In West African literature we find no books dealing specifically with the concept of blessing. Thus we shall have
to refer to brief sections in several books on Islam in
West Africa.

While the key books plus others give a great deal of insight into the concept of blessing, none of them has focused
on the relevancy of this concept for the church in its
mission today. Our study indicates the validity and
importance of the concept of blessing in the religion of
man in general, and in the faiths of Christianity, Judaism,
and Islam. It lies at the core of religion and thus needs
to be seriously considered by the Church in mission. It is
hoped that this study will be able to use the insights given
and indicate several relevant areas of potential use of
blessing in the Church.

II

Blessing in
Islam and Islamic Africa

The years 570-632 A.D. are strategic ones in the history of
the religion called Islam. They span the lifetime of Muhammad, the founder and promulgator of this new monotheistic
faith. The rapid rise in the influence and power of Islam
and its outreach from Spain to the Orient indicates that it
is a faith that readily deserves intense study. With belief
in the One True God (Allah) as the basis of this faith, and
the assertion that the Qur'an is the final and most complete
revelation of the tenets of true faith in God, Islam presents
to the world a fascinating, complex theology.

Because this study is considering the concept of blessing
with the aim of discovering its potential role in Christian
witness and ministry in West Africa, we must now explore the
basic aspects of this concept in Islam. As we deal with the
impact of blessing in Islam, we shall discover important
similarities with biblical material. This is understandable
because of the common Semitic heritage that Muslims, Jews,
and Christians have shared from their beginnings.

In Islam's holy book, the Qur'an, blessing is a basic,
pervasive concept. This fact may be one reason why few
scholars have focused their studies on this concept in Islam.
This lack of research does not mean that blessing is unim-
portant. On the contrary, its importance is evident by its
widespread use in greetings, praises, acclamations in the
lives of holy people, and as an attribute of God.

It is thus necessary that this study begin with an examination of blessing as presented in the basic structures of
Islam. This means exploring the use of blessing in the
Qur'an, seeing its impact in the life of Muhammad, and discovering its centrality in Sufism, the mysticism of Islam.
While various scholars may not include Sufism as a foundational aspect of Islam, we shall briefly deal with it because of its impact on the Islam of Africa.

After our introductory study, we shall examine blessing
in its African context. Even though our major concern is
with Islam in West Africa, we shall briefly review the Islam
of North Africa. We do so because there are a number of
similarities between the Islamic way of life in these two
regions of Africa. We shall discover specific ways in
which this dynamic force took root and projected itself
into the lives of Muslims living in these two vast regions
of Africa.

2

Blessing in the Foundations of Islam

From its birth in Arabia in the seventh century A.D., Islam has been a religion and faith of blessing. God was seen as a beneficient and benevolent power who gave his blessing to his followers and adherents.

DEFINING THE CONCEPT

A probing of the concept of blessing in Islam leads to two Arabic words used for blessing. *Salla* focuses on blessing, especially as it relates the blessing of the prophet Muhammad. But it is *baraka* that is the common and widespread word for blessing. If asked the Arabic word for blessing, a Muslim would almost always say "*baraka.*"

Salla

While the common definition of *salla* is "to pray," the word takes on the connotation of blessing when it is used to speak about Allah's divine favor on Muhammad. While Palmer (1900) translates Sura 33:56 as, "Verily, God and his angels pray for the prophet," (p. 148), most Muslims would not describe prayer as an activity of God. Thus, most translate this verse as Pickthall does: "Lo! Allah and His angels shower blessings on the Prophet. O ye who believe! Ask blessings on him and salute him with a worthy salutation" (Pickthall, 1953:306).

From this verse we see that *salla* is a greeting, a salutation. But it also includes the wish and desire for the pro-

tection and safekeeping of God. This is particularly true
when it is used by itself (Robson, 1936:368).

In addition, this sura indicates the wish for God to hon-
or the prophet. "God and angels honour and bless the holy
Prophet as the greatest of men. We are asked to honour and
bless him all the more because he took upon himself to suffer
the sorrows and afflictions of this life in order to guide
us to God's Mercy and the highest inner life" (Ali, 1946/2:
1125).

A common example of *salla* meaning "blessing" is the "tar-
teeb of salaat," part of the daily prayers that a Muslim
prays. After completing a second prostration, the Muslim
assumes a sitting position and prays the 'At-tahiyat:

> All good deeds and acts of worship are for the pleasure
> of Allah: O Holy Prophet, may Allah's blessing (*barakat*)
> and salutations be on your sacred soul, and on all the
> righteous servants of Allah: I bear witness that there
> is none worthy of worship except Allah, and that Mohammed
> is His servant and a Prophet.

While still sitting, the man or woman at prayer continues:

> O Allah! Bestow blessings on Mohammed (*Allahumma Salli
> 'ala Muhammadin*) and his descendants just as Thou didst
> bestow upon Abraham and his descendants, for Thou art the
> Praiseworthy and Exalted. O Allah! Exalt (*barik*-bless)
> Mohammed and his descendants, just as Thou didst exalt
> Abraham and his descendants, for Thou art the Praiseworthy
> and Exalted (Peerbhai, 1974:12-13).

Baraka

In Islam the universal word for blessing is *baraka*. *Baraka* is linguistically related to the Hebrew word *berakah*.
Thus, it is not unusual that theological meanings of the two
words are similar in many instances.

Divine virtue. One meaning of *baraka* is that of divine
virtue. God, in blessing his people, bestows upon certain
special believers an extra measure of benediction. These
holy people, often called saints, exude this divine virtue
in their lives so that other people come to them as a means
of being near God and in close relationship to Muhammad.
"The personal relationship of the believer to the Prophet
(is) through the *baraka* or 'virtue'" (Cragg, 1973:178).

This meaning of *baraka* is often emphasized in mystical cir-
cles of Muslims, such as the Sufis.

Cragg (1964) sees *baraka* being communicated primarily
through superstitious or magical forms. However, he views
superstition as a potential ground for valid faith. He
writes, "A similar parable of spiritual truth may be said
to attach to the idea of contact in *barakah*. This 'virtue'
or benison has to be had always by association, by touch, by
adjacence. It cannot be had without a personal relation between the desire and the supply, between the need and the
satisfaction" (Cragg, 1964:181).

Grace and mercy. A major meaning of *baraka* is grace and
mercy. As the benevolent creator and giver, God's primary
aim for his people is that they receive his grace and mercy.

For Muslims, the grace of God is the ultimate expression
of his blessing. Its splendors and virtues are greater than
any other gift. "Abul-Hasan al-Khirqani enjoins us to 'seek
the grace of God,' for it surpasses alike the terrors of
Hell and the delights of heaven" (Schuon, 1969:52fn). Yet,
baraka as grace is closely related to the natural order.
Muslims would not separate the natural order from the spiritual order. God is the giver, creator, and blesser of everything (Tabataba'i, 1975:27fn).

Baraka as mercy is the gift of God that works reconciliation between us and the Holy One. The concept of mercy is
especially strong in Sura 19, entitled Mary. Related closely
to the Magnificat (Luke 1:46-55), this sura's central theme
is the element of mercy. For Muslims, mercy is at one end of
a spectrum with demand for justice at the other end. Mercy
is what saves. Allah is called "Most Merciful and Compas-
sionate."

Protection. Most Muslims see the gift of *baraka* as God's
way of protecting them. Whether they are "popular" Muslims,
who possess amulets or other articles which supposedly contain power, or classical Muslims, they believe that the
blessing of God will prevent danger and trouble. Cragg
(1964) quotes a portion of Ahmad Amin's book entitled *Hayatu,
My Life.* The author is describing a lunch break which a Muslim teacher is taking with his students.

They dipped their hands for a mouthful, now into one
vessel, now into the other. Who bothered that they were
a motley mixture of all sorts and conditions, sick and

sound, dirty and clean, filthy and respectable. In God
was their trust and *barakah* obviated any danger (p. 145-
146).

Charisma. Blessing gives to the recipient of this gift of
God a special quality and power for charismatic leadership.
Whether he be a saint, scholar, or chief, a leader with *baraka* is greatly respected for his wisdom, influence, and
closeness to God.

Muhammad himself never claimed to be a special, almost
supernatural, person. He always was careful to highlight
his human nature. He claimed no power to work miracles, for
example. Yet he did not "deny being a bearer of that charismatic force, *baraka*, which his people as ancient and Eastern
peoples in general believed to reside in the extraordinary,
the saintly, personage" (Von Grunebaum, 1953:92).

It is particularly in the lives of saints, holy men, that
we see the emphasis of *baraka* as charisma. While the prom-
inence and emphasis on the power of the saints varies from
age to age and from area to area, most Muslims viewed them
and their *karamat* (charismatic gifts and power) as being
significant aspects of the Islamic faith.

Power. *Baraka* is understood also as divine power which
has semi-sacramental value. It is particularly evident in
one's devotional and meditational attitudes toward sacred
books, prayers, and people. The Qur'an has a great deal of
baraka, as do certain devotional prayer manuals. The Arabic
language is considered by Muslims as a holy language, God's
language. It is thus a conveyer of God's benevolent power.
As divine power, *baraka* protects and heals.

Each particular phrase of the devotional books has its
own *baraka*. "This sense of their practically independent
holy power ranges from the spiritual to the semi-magical.
It is at its strongest, of course, with any word from the
Qur'an and with the blessing on the Prophet" (Padwick, 1961:
xxvii).

The spark of the divine power of *baraka* is also attached
to holy people, and particularly to the Prophet. Padwick
(1961) includes a quote from a devotional manual of Uthman
al-Mirghani who prays to God with these words:

O God, call down blessing on our Lord Muhammad, and by his
baraka deliver us from the bane of the Arabs and the non-

Arabs and the bane of all thy creatures.... O God, call
down the blessing on our Lord Muhammad and by his *baraka*
deliver us from the bane of heat and cold, or rain and
wind.... And forgive us by his *baraka*...." (p. xxvi).

BLESSING IN THE QUR'AN

We have already stated that the Qur'an, in the estimation
of Muslims, is a sacred book, charged with *baraka*. They
view it as sacred not only because it is God's word, but
also because it bestows blessing. In this brief section, we
shall discuss how the word *baraka* is used in the Qur'an.

The word *baraka* is found 32 times in the Qur'an. The
noun form is used only in the plural (*barakat*). There are,
of course, other grammatical forms of the word. *Tabaraka* is
used frequently to glorify God. The participle *mubarak* describes persons or things upon whom God has conferred *baraka*
or the power to confer *baraka* (Gibb, 1962:189).

One finds several emphases and uses of blessing in the
Qur'an. Because God is considered to be the supreme source
of blessing, the Qur'an naturally expresses praise to him
for his blessing and his creative activity. Other targets
and aspects of blessing in the Qur'an are the land, the
Qur'an itself, greetings, fertility, and prayer. The Qur'an
also gives further insight into the essense of blessing itself.

Blessing as Praise of God

The most frequent use of *baraka* in the Qur'an is to praise
God. Usually the form used is that of the beatitude. God
is praised as the creator of the heavens and the earth (43:85;
25:61). He is called the "Best of Creators" (23:14). He is
praised for his sovereignty and Lordship (67:1; 7:54). He
is magnified because he gives the best (25:10) and provides
for the needs of the people (40:64). Because of the great-
ness of God's name, he is glorified (55:78).

Sura 25 contains three praises of God. The first verse
is a beatitude that summarizes or introduces the greatest
gift of God for which he is praised--the abundant goodness of
his revelation to Muhammad. In commenting on this beatitude,
Ali says: "Here that aspect of God's dealing with His creatures is emphasized, which shows His abundant goodness to all
His creatures, in that He sent the Revelation of His will,
not only in the unlimited Book of Nature, but in a definite

Book in human language, which gives clear directions and ad-
monitions to all" (Ali, 1946/2:926).

Blessing on the Land

The Qur'an reveals its Old Testament heritage in proclaiming the importance of the land. It speaks about the land
that Abraham and Lot were brought to as being "blessed for
all peoples" (21:17). This blessed land was the one to which
the pilgrim people journeyed (7:137) and which Solomon ruled
over (21:81). Jerusalem and the land of Israel are acclaimed as the "Far Distant Place of Worship" and are thus blessed by God (34:18). Also holy is Mecca, "the first Sanctuary
appointed for mankind...a blessed place, a guidance to the
peoples" (3:96).

The Blessed Qur'an

Three suras have references to the written revelation of
Allah as being a special blessing. It is labeled a special
Reminder (21:50). Often the messenger and the message are
inseparable. "Here is a Man and a Book, greater than Moses
and his book. Are you going to reject him and it?" (Ali,
1946/2:833).

For Muslims, the Qur'an is a book of blessing because it
gives people great truths upon which to meditate. In their
meditation they receive new insights and understandings.
Therefore, it is a book "full of blessing" (38:30).

Revelation is not a mere chance or haphazard thing. It
is a real blessing among the greatest that God has bestowed on man. By meditation on it in an earnest spirit
man may learn of himself, and his relation to nature
around him and to God the Author of all. Men of understanding may, by its help, resolve all genuine doubts
that there may be in their minds, and learn the true lessons of Spiritual life" (Ali, 1946/2:1224).

For Muslims, God's highest blessing is the guidance and
light which the Qur'an brings to them. This is because in
the meditating on and reading of the Qur'an, they come nearer
to God himself (6:93).

Creative Activity as Blessing

Not only does the Qur'an praise God as the creator of all
things, but it proclaims that various aspects of creation and

the creative activity of God are themselves blessings to the people. The nourishment of the earth (41:10) and the rain (blessed water--50:9) bring potential blessings of growth to the earth.

The most unusual creative activity of God as described in the Qur'an is found in Sura 19:31. Mary is described as bringing the baby Jesus in a cradle to her people. When asked to explain an event, she is at a loss for words. She simply points to the child who suddenly, through the creative activity of God, begins speaking. He explains who he is, a servant of God who has received a revelation from God which made him a prophet. "And he hath made me blessed wheresoever I may be."

It is interesting to note that the commentator Ali describes this event as a miracle in which Jesus defended his mother and preached to an unbelieving audience (Ali, 1946/2: 723). Yet in commenting on a similar verse, Sura 3:46, he seems to be struggling for support by stating that "some apocryphal Gospels describe him (Jesus) as preaching from infancy" (Ali, 1946/1:135).

Description of Blessing

Two verses in the Qur'an illuminate the concept of blessing in an Islamic context. Sura 7:96 describes *baraka* as being the result of faith and obedience. It is not for every man and woman, but only for those who come to a faith relationship with God and then continue in that relationship through obedience.

Sura 11:48 expands blessing to include grace and peace. Noah is invited to descend from the ark after the flood has subsided. He is greeted by God with the words of peace and promised the blessing of many descendants and a full measure of grace. In commenting on this event, Ali says:

Those who truly seek God's light and guidance and sincerely bend their will to His will are freely admitted to God's grace. Notwithstanding any human weaknesses in them, they are advanced higher in the spiritual stage on account of their Faith, Trust, and Striving after Right. They are given God's Peace, which gives the soul true calmness and strength, and all the blessings that flow from spiritual life (1946/1:526).

Thus we see that the concept of *baraka* is not only a vital teaching and aspect of the Qur'an, but it also is the power of the Qur'an. Muslims believe that this sacred book possesses *baraka* which preserves its power and impact so that it endures from generation to generation. The reading, memorizing, and chanting of the Qur'an is done by many Muslims. "That is done because the Divine presence in the text provides food for the souls of men. It is in fact a sacred act to recite the Qur'an. Its reading is a ritual act which God wishes man to perform over and over again throughout his earthly journey" (Nasr, 1966:52).

BLESSING IN THE LIFE OF MUHAMMAD

As one studies the documents which describe the life of Muhammad, one discovers two diverse attitudes in regard to *baraka* in his life. On the one hand are those realistic sources which see him as he saw himself, a human being chosen by God to bring renewal of faith in the One True God. On the other hand, there developed a vast array of devotional material which tended to build around Muhammad an aura of holiness and divine honor. It is these two different pictures which we shall explore in this section.

Blessing and Muhammad in the Qur'an

The Qur'an uses the personal name Muhammad only four times (Suras 3:138; 33:40; 47:2; and 48:29). This seems to indicate an attempt to downplay any approach of spiritualizing the Prophet. The Qur'an is insistent that Muhammad is only human. His task is that of a humble messenger (3:138; 17:92). As said earlier, the Qur'an claims that no miracles were performed by Muhammad. In fact, Jesus is praised more and given more titles and power in the Qur'an than is Muhammad.

Yet, throughout the Qur'an one reads of the close relationship between Allah and Muhammad. There is a strong link between the two at every point, "whether in claims to obedience, in warnings, in tests of loyalty, in activity" (Cragg, 1964:200). Both God and the angels bless the Prophet (33:56).

All this indicates that God gave Muhammad a special measure of blessing. It is seen in the charisma which was characteristic of the leadership he had that was necessary to accomplish the revolution he brought about and to overcome the numerous obstacles he faced.

Blessing and Muhammad in Popular Devotional Material

Because of the close relationship between God and Muhammad which is recited daily in the *shahadah*--"There is no god but God (Allah), and Muhammad is the prophet (messenger) of God"--there developed in many Muslim communities a deepening veneration toward the Prophet. In celebrating every major transition in Muhammad's life, Muslims devotionally ascribed praise and blessing to the Prophet.

We see an example of this in the *Maulid* poems (quoted by Cragg, 1964:201). The poet highlights the *baraka* of Muhammad as he is:

praised as the fairest rose in creation, the splendour of the sun in strength. In his hands is a fountain of waters: his body is radiant and his wonders continue to the end of time. His father Abdallah, sought his bride, the Prophet's mother, with prayers and when he found her she shone in his eyes like a pearl. On the night of a Friday in Rajab when Muhammad was conceived, God ordered that Paradise should be opened and angelic voices announced the coming one.

In such devotional material, both Muhammad's conception and birth are viewed as being permeated with *baraka*. This is accepted as a divine power inherent in his life as a young orphan. A story which illustrates devotion to Muhammad recounts the occasion when Muhammad is taken by foster parents after his father died. When the neighbors of the new foster mother ridicule her, she answers, "By God, I have taken the fairest babe that I ever saw, and he with the greatest *baraka*" (Rodinson, 1971:45).

Devotional literature also ascribes miraculous power to Muhammad. It claims that one sign that indicated he possessed *baraka* was that he made water spring from between his fingers. He was also able to multiply food because of this divine power. These two accounts are part of the traditions recorded by Dirini, an Egyptian mystic (Rodinson, 1971:304).

Jeffery (1962) has compiled *A Reader on Islam* in which he includes selected Islamic devotional material. Among the selections one finds "The Miracles of the Prophet," a part of the *Sira*, and "A Litany of Blessings on the Prophet." In the latter the prayer repeats over and over the phrase, "Allahumma, grant blessings to our Lord Muhammad."

All this indicates that, for Muslims, there is a deep
spiritual significance in the life and blessings of Muhammad.
While the degree to which *baraka* and divine power ascribed
to him will vary, all Muslims maintain that Muhammad was
richly and divinely blessed by God and made the one who received the final and most complete revelation of truth.
Nasr (1966) believes that one reason why many non-Muslims
have difficulty grasping the impact of blessing in the life
of Muhammad:

> is that the spiritual nature of the Prophet is veiled in
> his human one and his purely spiritual function is hidden
> in his duties as the guide of men and the leader of a
> community. It was the function of the prophet to be not
> only a spiritual guide, but also the organizer of a new
> social order with all that such a function implies. And
> it is precisely this aspect of his being that veils his
> purely spiritual dimension from foreign eyes (p. 68).

BLESSING IN SUFISM

Another foundational element of Islam where blessing is
a key aspect is that of Sufism. Sufism is the mystical
movement within Islam. While there are many different facets
to Sufism upon which one can focus one's attention (and
there are extremes that many orthodox Sufis reject), one can
generally say that Sufists aim to probe the mystery and revelation of God.

A Sufi is a Muslim who seeks mystical union with God.
This usually means that Sufism is true asceticism, separation
from the world, and basking in the divine love of God.

> Divine love makes the seeker capable of bearing, of even
> enjoying, all the pains and afflictions that God showers
> upon him in order to test him and purify the soul. This
> love can carry the mystic's heart to the Divine Presence
> 'like a falcon which carries away the prey,' separating
> him, thus, from all that is created in time (Schimmel,
> 1975:4).

A Sufi affirms that he has a direct relationship with God.
Due to his close relationship with God, he receives spiritual power and blessing (*baraka*) from God. Because each Sufi's
encounter with God is different, we find a wide variety of
expressions and uses of *baraka* among Sufis. Yet they have
many characteristics in common.

Foundation of Sufism in Muhammad and the Qur'an.

A major claim of Sufism is that its origin is in the Qur'an and in the life of Muhammad. Sufists would affirm that "Muhammad was a Sufi when on his way to be a prophet" (Macdonald, 1903:227). Both in his lifestyle and in his teachings, Muhammad revealed a tendancy toward mysticism and asceticism. He asserted that poverty and abstinence were marks of a true Muslim. This led to a strong rigid emphasis on prayer, fasting, and other forms of self-discipline. The hope was that through these exercises a believer would come very close to God. Some Sufi extremists heretically believed that one could even attain absorption into God.

The Qur'an contains numerous passages of a mystical character and gives avid support to the lifestyle of Sufism. Sufis eagerly point out several Qur'anic verses which support their claim of being close to God. For example, "And when My servants question thee concerning Me, then surely I am nigh. I answer the prayer of the supplicant when he crieth unto Me. So let them hear my call and let them trust in Me, in order that they may be led aright" (Sura 2:186). "We verily created a man and We know what his soul whispereth to him, and We are nearer to him than his jugular vein (Sura 50:16).

The Qur'an also contains many passages on prayer, fasting, continuous worship of God, and other forms of self-discipline. Unworldliness is set before the believer as a great virtue. "Know that the life of this world is only play, and idle talk, and pageantry, and boasting among you, and rivalry in respect of wealth and children.... (Sura 57:20). "This life of the world is but a pastime and a game... (Sura 29:64).

There is ample evidence to indicate that Islamic mysticism was influenced by Christian mystical teachings and monastic practices. But it was Muhammad and the Qur'an that laid the foundation "of a doctrine of mysticism, based on asceticism, which was further developed by the early Traditionalists and later became that fully-developed system of Islamic mysticism which we know as Sufism" (Smith, 1976:152).

Expressions of Blessing in Sufism

As Sufism developed in the history of Islam, it encountered resistance from the strict, orthodox, legal interpreters of Islam. Sufis claimed to possess knowledge of the

Truth (*al-Haqq*), which orthodox Muslims said could only be
gained through revealed religion (Qur'an). They reacted
against the Sufis making use of intuitive and emotional experiences rather than the intellect. A Muslim reacting
against Sufism would say something like, "All that we need
for salvation we can hold in our hand. Why get the heart
involved?"

In the development of Sufi teaching and practice, we see
the beginnings of "popular" Islam which stresses the importance of individual saints, holy lineages, and holy orders
and brotherhoods. The concept of blessing is a key factor
in the impact and influence each has made on the world of
Islam.

Becoming a Sufi saint. One of the most persistent doctrines of Sufism is inwardness. Instead of focusing on the
external rituals of Islam, they shift their emphasis to inward worship, service, and the brotherhood of man. A vital
aspect of this mystical inwardness is contact with and reception of *baraka*, the divine favor, blessing, and power of
God. While this potent force seems similar to animistic
baraka, for true Sufists it is clearly different (Chelhod,
1955:68). Those who acquire a great deal of *baraka* through
mystical union with God become known as saints.

At this point it is necessary that a proper distinction
be made between Christian saints and Muslim saints. For
Protestants, a saint, in general, is a Christian. He is a
member of the Communion of Saints, the Church. A Protestant
often reacts negatively to the sacred, miraculous realm of
sainthood. This has resulted in a Protestant saint being
"merely an abstract embodiment of sanctity and divine pro-
venience" (Turner, 1974:59).

Roman Catholicism developed a rigid procedure for the
recognition of saints. Only the Pope eventually could canon-
ize a person as a saint. The saint was presented by the
Pope as a subject of honor and veneration. This means that
death must occur before a holy person can be correctly called
a saint. Because becoming a saint means acquiring a great
deal of grace and exhibiting an orthodox theology, most
Roman Catholic saints were former monks, nuns, and theologians.

But in Islam, one becomes a saint through the power and
charisma he receives from God and exhibits in his life. A
Muslim saint possesses *baraka* which gives him power to per-

form miracles and other "supernatural" feats. Because there
is no central authority in Islam (other than the Qur'an and
Muhammad), the acceptance of a person as a saint is not primarily based on orthodox theology. Rather it is orthopraxy
that is the determining factor in one's being acclaimed a
saint.

For Islam in general, and Sufism in particular, a saint
is one who is somehow "in touch with that *barakah* which runs
through the arteries of the universe" (Nasr, 1972:50). Sufi
saints see their achievement of integration as resulting in
a contact with this cosmological, yet personal, *baraka* of
God. This, in turn, means that they are charged with this
power of grace. Thus, we see that a person can become a
saint, a bearer of blessing, by his intimate contact with
God.

Inheriting blessing. However, personal contact with God
was not the only way to become a saint in past years. Through
one's lineage one could inherit *baraka*. If a descendant of
Muhammad inherited an extraordinary measure of blessing, he
was called a saint (*wali, siyyid*). The most highly respected and recognized saints always traced their *baraka* back
through their ancestry to the Prophet himself. "In Sufism,
in order to gain access to the methods which alone make
spiritual realisation possible, man must become attached to
an initiatory chain of *silsilah* which goes back to the Prophet and through which a barakah flows from the source of
the revelation to the being of the initiate. The chain is
thus based on a continuity of spiritual presence....(Nasr,
1972:112). In some ways this is similar to the concept of
apostolic succession in the Roman Catholic Church and in
some Protestant churches.

Because of the Islamic belief in the transferability of
baraka, Sufi saints bestowed this power in several ways.
Because his body was blessed with *baraka*, the clothing he
wore became charged with this power. The Sufis were identified by the patched frock they wore (most scholars believe
they got their name from this course woolen material--*suf*).
If the wool clothing was touched by a person, *baraka* was
transferred from the saint to him.

The prestige of *baraka* was especially strong among the
masses. People sought out the saints when they had particular problems or needs. They believed that anything possessed by or coming from a saint contained *baraka*. "It is
not enough for them to see him and acclaim him; they almost

all hope to touch him if they can, or at least touch objects
which belong to him...in order to soak up the Sharifian
baraka" (Le Tourneau, 1955:247). An extreme example of this
fervor for the *baraka* of saints is seen in the testimony of
the Persian saint Abu Sa'id who said, "One day when I was
riding on horseback, my horse dropped dung. Eager to gain
a blessing, the people came and picked up the dung and
smeared their heads and faces with it" (Nicholson, 1921:16).

While one could question the validity of such *baraka* as
coming from God, it indicates the intensity of the people
in their search for communion with God and his power and
grace. They believed that many of the acts of faith bestow
this divine favor and blessing. The pilgrimage to Mecca is
especially beneficient in the bestowal of blessing. Many
Muslims also make regular visits to the tombs of Muslim
saints. This is because, strictly speaking, Muslim saints
and marabouts never really die; they merely slumber in their
tombs. The tomb thus became an oasis of blessing for gen-
erations to come. In many Muslim countries where Sufism is
strong, the countryside is dotted with sacred tombs.

Holy orders of saints. We have seen that a Muslim can
become a saint through individual contact with and total devotion to God through which he receives God's blessing. A
person can also inherit blessing and become a saint. But
there is a third way in which an aspirant can attain sainthood. This way is by studying in Sufi schools of mysticism
and joining holy orders.

Called *tariqa*, these mystical, monastic type religious
orders developed a novitiate system and secret initiations
through which one could enter the order. Each order and
school was led by a shaikh or marabout who supervised the
teaching, prayers, spiritual exercises, and growth of the
apprentices. The orders were often associated with particular tombs and the veneration of saints. In fact, "no clear
distinction can henceforth be made between the orders and
saint-veneration, since God's proteges (*awliya' li'llah*) are
within the orders" (Trimingham, 1971:26).

These holy orders, or brotherhoods as they are sometimes
called, are especially prevalent in North and West Africa.
To see their impact and influence in these large regions of
Africa, we shall now turn our attention to Islam in Africa,
beginning with North Africa.

3

Blessing in Islamic North Africa

In studying the concept of blessing in North Africa, we come face to face with the drama of the interaction of the divine and the human, the sacred and the profane, the holy and the secular. The consequence of such interaction and encounter is shaped by the particular cultural, social, and historical context in which the phenomenon takes place. While the scope of this study prevents us from doing a thorough historical survey of the manifestation of blessing in North African Islam, we will briefly discuss particular examples and models which show how this interaction developed in several key areas and how it influenced Islam in West Africa.

In the fusion of the divine and the human, the concept of blessing grew and became influential in three major related institutional contexts. It was the variety of cultural settings which took this common concept of divine favor and blessing and portrayed it in various forms, what Geertz (1968: 49) calls "complexes." These three religious institutional settings are the *siyyid* complex, a cult of saints centered around their tombs; the *zawiya* complex, religious orders or brotherhoods; and the *makhzen* complex, the sultan (monarch-traditional government) and the cult centered around him.

THE VENERATION OF SAINTS

The first of the trilogy of institutional complexes is the *siyyid* complex. Growing out of Sufi mysticism, the *siyyid* became a vast network of tribalized worship centers. Though Muslims who participated in the veneration of saints were

quick to point out that the "worship" of saints was always
less significant than the adoration of God, they still believed in its efficacy. They did not let the negative reaction of some strict orthodox Muslims prevent them from
being a part of this aspect of Islam.

The saints (*wali, siyyid*) were special holy people who
inherited the power of blessing through intimate contact with
God or through sacred lineages. Through their heritage (many
could trace their ancestry back to the Prophet), many saints
received *baraka* and were viewed as mediators between God and
man. Most Muslims had great respect for and belief in the
power of the saints. The intensity of the people's devotion to the saints is seen in the words of Shaikh Muhi al-Din
ibn 'Arabi in his *Meccan Revelations:* "The highest happiness
of men is to believe in all those who ascribe to themselves
a relationship with God, even if this claim were not justi-
fied" (Goldziher, 1971:267-68).

In North Africa, the recognition of a saint was a local,
often tribal, phenomenon. A person's claim to saintship
depended primarily on his manifesting an intimate relationship with God. This took on many forms, such as charismatic
leadership, fits of ecstacy, and, above all, the ability to
work miracles. These *karamat* (charismatic gifts) combined
with the claim of being a descendant of the Prophet led Muslims to come to saints to receive their blessing. The fact
that the veneration of saints was also a pre-Islamic phenomenon made the area fertile ground for this developing Islamic
concept (Douglas, 1948:267).

The major characteristic of the *siyyid* complex is the
veneration of the saints after their "death." The elements
of this primarily rural institution include:

> first, the tomb and its associated paraphernalia; second,
> the saint supposedly buried in the tomb; third, the living
> patrilineal descendants of the saint; and fourth, the cult
> by means of which the baraka embodied in the tomb, the
> saint, and the descendants are made available for human
> purposes (Geertz, 1968:49).

In North Africa, the rural landscape is dotted with squat,
white-domed crypts. Because of the *baraka* associated with
them, many Muslims make periodic pilgrimages to these tombs.
They believe that the saints' graves are inviolable sanctuaries. Some of them have become noted for being especially
holy and powerful. Many are specialized in that they are

effective in ministering to particular needs. A few of them
are so significant that some Muslims believe that a pilgrimage made to them would take the place of the *hajj*, the required pilgrimage to Mecca. This is particularly true if
the *hajj* is extremely difficult or impossible.

Burke (1973) describes one of these sepulchres on a trip
he took with a Muslim across the Tunisian desert. From
time to time he and his companion, Hamid, passed a white dome
over the tomb of a saint.

One tomb was in a depression, where some water had man-
aged to make its way to the surface, even to nourish a
single palm tree. Beneath the tree several stakes were
standing; from each one a number of knotted rags hung
limply. "Is it true that these rags are tied there as a
reminder to the saint to help people who make a visit to
the shrine, that he may help them in some supernatural
way?" "No," said Hamid. "You are wrong. Absolutely."
"Then what are they there for?" "They are pieces of gar-
ments which have been worn by supplicants. The *baraka*,
the inner power and blessing, of the Sheikh who is buried
in the tomb forms a link with the essence of the person
whose garment this was. By this means the *baraka* is
transmitted to the sufferer." "Irrespective of distance,
and the time which has elapsed since the death of the
Sheikh?" "That is so." "Where was I wrong?" "You were
wrong in thinking that they reminded the Sheikh of anything. They merely contact the *baraka* which suffuses the
surroundings" (P. 41).

As Geertz mentioned, those who adore the saints and their
tombs do not believe that the saint is really dead. This is
not surprizing when one realizes that many Muslims believe
that the dead recognize a fellow Muslim who is near his tomb.
Ibn al-Qaiyim maintains that "the dead man hears the beating
of the sandals of those who say farewell to him, when they
leave him. The Prophet prescribed a law for his people, that
they should greet the people of the graves as they would
greet one with whom they were talking face to face, one endowed with the powers of hearing and reason" (Cooke, 1935:
131). If there is belief in communication with all the dead,
how much more significant is the communication with a saint!
A major reason for this communication was the appropriation
of blessing. People wanted to receive this divine power of
God so that they could better cope with the problems facing
them in their daily lives.

MARABOUTS AND THEIR MINISTRY IN THE RELIGIOUS ORDERS

The second way in which the divine reveals itself in the
Islamic world of North Africa is through the *tariqa*. *Tariqa*
is the term which is applied to the numerous Islamic orders
and brotherhoods. The location where the orders met is
called the *zawiya*. The *zawiya* quickly became a retreat center, a lodge, where Muslims could gather for sharing and
growth. They usually are located in the urban centers and
the towns.

It is in the *zawiya* that those blessed with an extra measure of charisma are chosen and recognized as "marabouts."
This French word comes from the Arabic *murabit*. It means to
tie, bind, fasten, attach, hitch, moor. A marabout is thus
a man that is tied, bound, fastened--perhaps the best word is
"shackled to God" (Geertz, 1968:43). The concept of marabout thus overlaps that of saint. The role of the marabout
is one of the most striking features of Islam in North
Africa because he is revered as having a special relationship
with God.

It is in the context of the marabout and his role in the
tariqa that we can best understand the impact and role of
baraka. "No context is given which allows a more precise
understanding of *baraka*, its recognition or transmission,
the importance attached to claims of geneological descent,
or other issues which could clarify the significance of
marabouts in Moroccan society" (Eickelman, 1976:37).

The *baraka* of the marabout is evident in several aspects
of his ministry. First, he is viewed by most, if not all
adherents of his brotherhood, as a mediator between God and
man. This is particularly significant when one realizes that
there is a wide gap between a literate God, whose prime
characteristic for Muslims is that he has revealed himself in
a book, and illiterate rural peasants. It is the personage
of the marabout whose mediation bridges the gap. As mediators, the marabouts "embody a literate religious message in
their dance, poetry, and symbolism" (Turner, 1974:69). In
communicating the message of Islam, the marabouts bring the
people into a closer relationship with God whose blessings
they crave. The *zawiya* center thus becomes a religious
renewal center and school through which knowledge, power, and
faith are bestowed.

But the *zawiya* is more than a religious center. It also
has social and political functions. In more remote towns

and villages that are far from the central government, the
religious brotherhood center serves as a welfare, commercial,
and political agency. Although these multiple functions
diminish in importance as services of national governments
become more comprehensive, one can say that in many areas
of North Africa, even today, the *zawiya* is "simultaneously
a religious nook, a solicitor's office and a mutual aid
society" (Turner, 1974:69).

The fact that the marabouts fulfill these diverse functions indicates that the concept of *baraka* is not viewed only
in vertical terms. It is not only a spiritual power of
blessing. It is also seen as a form of causality. It is
believed to have an impact on nature as well. Things which
have been said to possess *baraka* include: marabouts, tribes,
tombs, twins, pregnant women, certain animals (especially
horses and sheep), plants, writings, planets, days, numbers,
names, and places. Westermarck (1926) takes three chapters
to describe the vast numbers of items which are believed to
possess *baraka*.

Westermarck describes *baraka* as a "mysterious wonder-work-
ing force which is looked upon as a blessing from God"
(Westermarck, 1926/1):35). He portrays *baraka* as being
closely related to both blessing and cursing, to both sanctity and impurity. "The case is similar when a person who
is possessed of *baraka* pronounces a curse or inflicts some
other injury. His *baraka* helps him carry out his curse or
evil intention" (Westermarck, 1926/1:219). While acknowledg-
ing Westermarck's understanding of *baraka*, one could question
his relating this power with both blessing and cursing. One
could ask whether *baraka* used to curse has its source in God.

Correspondingly, the Islamic understanding of *baraka* is
not magic either, as Doutté (1909) infers. One could easily
come to Doutté's conclusion upon viewing the significant role
of the miraculous in the ministry of the marabout in the *zawiya*. However, true Islam insists that the power to work miracles is a blessing of God. This does not ignore the fact
that in some cultural settings which have had great animistic
influences that a certain magical element may have become
part of the belief in and understanding of *baraka*.

In North Africa the *tariqa* brotherhoods have a great deal
of variety. This is generally a result of the influence of
local cultures. Each brotherhood or order has certain unique
characteristics. The range of ceremonial practices that are
significant aspects of the group range from "simple bead-

telling repetition of the names of God, through blood sacrifice, to the more famous sort of whirling dervish per-
formances--dancing with swords, playing with fire, charming
snakes, mutual flagellation, and so on" (Geertz, 1968:52).
Each *zawiya* had its peculiar rites, procedures, methods, or
ways of accomplishing its tasks. It was this liturgical and
symbolic process that guarded the brotherhood's unity and
retained its unique identity.

But whatever the particular characteristics, each *zawiya*
complex had a marabout as spiritual leader. This holy sheikh
was the chief possessor and communicator of *baraka*. It was
this divine force that held the brotherhood together down
through history and served as the attraction which continuously drew new adherents to its fellowship.

As said earlier, the particular format and uniqueness of
a religious brotherhood was usually due to historical and
cultural reasons. To get a better picture of the diversity
and impact of these *tariqa* orders, we shall briefly describe
three representative ones in North Africa. We shall look at
Shadhiliyya, Tijaniyya, and Sanusiyya.

Shadiliyya

The order of Shadhiliyya was the earliest *tariqa* to stem
out of North African soil and is recognized as one of the
most important ones in that area. Named after its founder,
Abu 'l-Hasan 'Ali ash Shadhili (1196-1258), it became the
"mother" order of many later brotherhoods.

As a young man, Shadhili became versed in both the general
sciences and the mystical sciences. He found a spiritual
master in "Abd al-Salem bin Mashish of Morocco. This Sufi
teacher "recognized the 'saintly' qualities of the young man
and gave him his final injunction to refrain from men and to
depart to Tunisia" (Douglas, 1948:269).

Thus, Shadhili became an ascetic, a traveling mendicant.
He devoted much time to fasting and prayer. He became known
as a miracle worker, even claiming to be able to change iron
into gold. Due to his *karamat*, the number of his followers
increased sharply. This caused concern in some local governmental officials, so Shadhili moved to Egypt.

In Egypt Shadhili became known for his piety. He established a *zawiya* there and was well accepted by most people.
Even the renowned secular scientists of his area, who nor-

mally frowned on Sufi mysticism, had great respect for Shadhili (Trimingham, 1971;48).

Theologically, Shadhili was known for his ability to balance orthodoxy with mysticism, a feat seldom accomplished by
Sufi mystics. While he affirmed the articles of faith of
Islam, he focused his proclamation on the individual's relationship with God. Real faith meant turning the heart away
from everything except God.

Shadhili did not purposefully organize a *tariqa*. He
strongly encouraged his followers to pursue their trade or
profession, but also to combine it with acts of devotion.
The five principles of his system of devotion were:

1) Fear of Allah in secret and open; 2) adherence to the
Sunna in words and deeds; 3) contempt of mankind in prosperity and adversity; 4) resignation to the will of Allah
in things great and small; 5) having recourse to Allah
in joy and sorrow (Margoliouth, 1965:509).

The Shadhili brotherhood has become known for its submission to governmental authorities and aloofness from tem-
poral affairs. Its worship is primarily the recitation of
special litanies (*dhikr*). Meaning "remembrance," *dhikr* are
set phrases and prayers through which one glorifies God by
stating various acts of remembrances. One may say these
litanies verbally or silently. The aim of the repetition of
the *dhikr* is to lose one's consciousness in mystical union
with God (Douglas, 1948:276).

Dhikr is as important to Sufists as love is to Christians.
"It is the Qoranic use of the cognitive term 'remembrance,'
rather than 'love' which has, perhaps more than anything else,
imposed on Islamic mysticism its special terminology" (Lings,
1971:45).

The Shadhili order claims to have three peculiarities or
specialties which make it distinct from other orders.
These are:

1) That they were all chosen from the "well-guarded Tab-
let," i.e., have been destined from all eternity to belong to it; 2) that ecstasy with them is followed by sob-
riety, i.e., does not permanently incapacitate them from
active life; 3) that the *qutb* (the highest spiritual leader of all Sufis) will always be one of them (Margoliouth,
1965:509-10).

Tijaniyya.

The Tijaniyya order or brotherhood was founded by Ahmad al-Tijani (1737-1817). He felt the call to Sufism at the age of 21. He began visiting several sheikhs, especially those located in Fez, Morocco. He was initiated into the Khalwatiyya order and became a teacher. However, during a pilgrimage to Mecca, he encountered an Indian sheikh. This man informed al-Tijani that he was to become a *qutb*. Two brief months later this Indian sheikh died and Tijani is said to have "inherited all his occult mystical learning" (Abun-Nasr, 1965:18).

He returned to North Africa and eventually set up his own order with his *zawiya* at Fez, Morocco. His claim to be the *qutb* of all Sufism naturally did not sit well with other Sufi orders and sheikhs. Many learned orthodox Muslims branded the order as heretical.

The Tijaniyya order has many peculiarities which distinguish it from other orders. Al-Tijani made no claim, as other sheikhs usually did, of being part of the *silsila*, the chain of authority through which *baraka* flowed from the Prophet to the sheikh. Instead, al-Tijani claimed to have a direct revelation and sanction of his position when the Prophet appeared to him while awake, instructed him in the litanies (*dhikr*), and the number of times they were to be repeated. Thus one could say that al-Tijani "produced a one-link *silsila* which went directly from him to the Prophet" (Abun-Nasr, 1965:38).

Because of his insistence that his followers trust and accept him as the chief sheikh of all Sufism, members of the Tijaniyya order are not allowed to belong to any other order. In fact, they are prohibited from visiting any other saint or saint's tomb. The brotherhood requires complete devotion and strict obligatory observance of the prescribed rites and the recitation of the litanies. Tijaniyya was to become the final word in Sufism, just as Islam was to become the final revelation in religion.

The Tijaniyya order is also unique in that it is anti-ascetic. The members are noted for their love of luxury. They look with disfavor on Sufi orders that pride themselves on poverty and dependence on charity for survival.

In the next chapter we shall discover that the Tijaniyya order functioned somewhat differently in West Africa. Yet its basic doctrines and emphases remained basically the same.

Sanusiyya

The final Sufi order in North Africa which we shall discuss is the Sanusiyya order. It is included because it was
a vital part of the renewal movement in the 19th and 20th
centuries and because of its penetration into West Africa.
Being one of the later orders to develop, it became a revi-
valistic movement within Islam. Martin (1976:99) calls it
"a halfway house between traditional Sufism and Wahhabi reform." Its influences reached across the Sahara to West
Africa in the Chad area. With its main center in Libya, the
order was politically active and served as a mediator in
political disputes. It pushed for Libyan nationalism which,
paradoxically, was a key factor in its overthrow and sup-
pression in 1969.

The founder of the Sanusiyya order was Muhammad 'Ali as-
Sanusi (1787-1859). After extended study at Fez, where he
became occupied with studies in law and politics in addition
to Islamic mysticism, he made a pilgrimage to Mecca. He remained there for thirteen years, during which time he was
greatly influenced by a supreme Sufi master, Ahmad ibn Idris
al-Fasi from Morocco, the founder of the Ahmadiya-Idrisiya
order. Al-Fasi was much like al-Tijani in that he claimed
to receive guidance and *baraka* directly from Muhammad. Al-
Fasi rejected the typical Sufi emphasis of mystical union
with God, but substituted for it mystical union with the
Prophet.

Al-Fasi and as-Sanusi (called the Grand Sanusi) became
intimate companions. A few years later al-Fasi died. This
led as-Sanusi to build a *zawiya* near Mecca. But turmoil in
the area caused him to return to North Africa. There he
established a center at Bayda in Cyrenaica (eastern Libya).
It was an excellent choice in that it was located in a political vacuum, isolated from turmoil in the west and the
north (with the Ottoman Turks). Yet this isolation tended
to increase the order's emphasis on remaining somewhat aloof
from normal life. Later important centers were built at
Kufra and Jaghbub. After his death, the Grand Sanusi was
succeeded by his son al-Mahdi.

The Sanusi order is known for its strong emphasis on re-
turning to pure Islamic teaching. While maintaining the
tenets of Sufism (he proudly spoke of the *baraka* he received
through his lineage from the Prophet), Sanusi stressed a high
moral and ethical standard that was based on the Qur'an and
Sunna.

   The order and its leaders also worked hard to achieve
unity in Islamic thought, worship, and action (Trimingham,
1971:120). Because of this philosophy, the order considered
all Muslims, whether they belonged to other orders or not, as
possible converts to their way of thinking. This naturally
led to some antagonism on the part of learned Muslims and
Islamic organizations.

   In spite of its stress on escape from the world, the Sanusi order was one of the most missionary-oriented of all
Sufi orders. While refusing to use the *jihad* (holy war) as
a means of evangelism, they were known to be strongly anti-
Christian and anti-Jewish. Because the French were ruling
Algeria at the time, the Sanusi order shifted its expansion
focus to the south. They constructed new *zawiya* centers as
they expanded their influence. In West Africa they became
strong in Chad, northern Cameroon, and even thrust as far
west as Kano, Nigeria in the 1890's (Martin, 1976:119). However, over a decade later they encountered fierce French
opposition in the Chad area and thus were forced to retreat
northward.

   In summary, we can say that the Sanusi order was a reviv-
alist movement within Islam that tried to help its followers
live like Muslims of the 7th century in the context of the
19th and 20th centuries. Because of this, it became somewhat
unrealistic in its outlook on life. "It found itself completely incompatible with the more recent developments of
affairs--political, social, economic, and intellectual. Its
teachings are incapable of expanding themselves so as to
include modern civilization" (Ziadeh, 1958:134).

   In spite of this negative evaluation, the Sansui order remained a valid option for Muslim Sufis. Its strongest asset
was its internal organization. Its *zawiya* centers served as
key participants in maintaining tribal unity in the areas it
served. Its strong emphasis on organization is a key to
better understanding the brotherhoods found in West Africa.
Evans-Pritchard (1949) writes:

   Unlike the heads of most Islamic orders, which have rapid-
   ly disintegrated into autonomous segments without contact
   and common direction, they (Sanusi) have been able to
   maintain this organization intact and keep control of it.
   This they were able to do by coordinating the lodges of
   the Order to the Tribal structure (p. 11).

THE SULTANATE AND ITS CULT

The third major institutional form in which we see the dynamic role of blessing at work is the *mahkzen* complex. This is the traditional term for the central sherifian government, centered in the sultan. This form is particularly strong in Morocco. Because of the claim that he and his ancestors were descendants of the Prophet, and because he was viewed as possessing a great deal of charisma, there developed a royal cult to enhance his position and prestige.

The sultan's primary religious tasks were to preserve and expand the role of Islamic scholarship, set special days for religious festivals, appoint Islamic judges, and guard the veneration of saints. The masses viewed the sultan as more than a governmental official. He was a holy man who was the accepted leader, worthy of adoration.

Makhzen is the term used for the staff of the sultan. The people believed that they as well as the sultan were charged with *baraka*. In this way they were venerated much like ascetic saints and leaders of orders. The religious cult revealed this attitude of the people toward the sultan. For example, the pronouncement of the sermon on Friday was done in the Sultan's name (Geertz, 1968:53).

Because the sultan and the *makhzen* had dual roles, political and religious, they often experienced conflict. The political role clashed with the religious one and tended to dominate it. Without the religious cult to support them, the sultan and his staff would have lost all vestiges of religious power and charisma.

In Morocco, where the sultanate is predominant, the monarchy is the key institution in Islam. This is due to the unique ability of being able to paradoxically combine two opposite streams of influence. On the one hand, a person is chosen ruler because he demonstrates an inner charisma (*baraka*) which he has inherited from his lineage. Because of this factor, he is viewed as a spiritual leader who is supernaturally qualified to be one.

But, at the same time, there is the political factor involved in choosing a leader. He must be chosen by the community, by his political comrades. There must be collective agreement as to his leadership and spokesmanship abilities.

Somehow, both of these factors are involved in the selec-
tion of the sultan. Both are legitimate reasons for a person being chosen as sultan. Geertz (1968) summarizes the
amazing complex this way:

> On the one hand, the Sultan was the chief marabout of the
> country, the ranking saint; his authority was spiritual.
> On the other hand, the Sultan was the duly chosen leader
> of the Islamic community, its officially appointed head;
> his authority was political. And what is more amazing,
> these two concepts of what the Sultan was were not equal-
> ly diffused throughout the society: his sacredness was
> universally recognized, or virtually so, but his sover-
> eignty most definitely was not. He reigned everywhere
> but he ruled only in places (p. 77).

CONCLUDING REMARKS

In all three of the major institutional complexes--the
individual saints, the orders, and the sultanate,--the
concept of blessing was a determining and basic factor. It
could be achieved through close contact with God and/or
through inheritance. It was viewed by Sufis and by the
masses as a mysterious supernatural power that could be
transferred to them. While true Sufis never lost sight of
the truth that blessing had its source in God, there was a
tendency for some to forget that fact in their religious
fervor and enthusiasm to receive this divine force and favor.

The concept of blessing played a dynamic role in both
the political and religious life of the people. While its
manifestation in Sufism was viewed with a degree of disdain
by strict orthodox Muslims, its impact on the spread of Islam
and the direction its expansion took is immeasurable. The
concept of blessing (*baraka*) in North Africa played a significant role in the expansion of Islam in West Africa and
the style of Islamic life there.

4

Blessing in
Islamic West Africa

The Muslim community sees mission as one of its directives
from God. Thus, it is not surprising to discover messengers
of Islam following the trade routes from the Maghrib across
the formidable Sahara Desert to the savannah Sahel region of
West Africa. As Muslim commercial enterprises became established in key centers on the edge of the desert, Islamic
teachers made the trek from the Mediterranean shores to the
ever-changing chain of West African empires.

Islam in West Africa was influenced to a great extent by
the Islam of North Africa. One finds many similarities between the two. Yet the Islam that became prominent in West
Africa also has several forms and emphases that are different from that of North Africa. This is mainly due to the
fact that traditional African religions accepted only certain elements of Islam while stubbornly resisting others.

The most noticeable difference is the lack of the phenomenon of veneration of saints. In North Africa the Muslim
masses throng to the tombs of the saints to acquire the *baraka* emanating from them. The primary connotation of *baraka*
in North Africa is divine force, power, and healing grace.

In West Africa one does not discover as much of this aspect of Islam. While the adoration of saints may have been
a meaningful experience for the Berbers and the Moors and
other North African peoples, there is a general consensus
that the veneration of saints is a contradiction to the view
of life after death of West Africans (Martenson, 1977:35).

47

In West Africa the cult of the ancestors is not tied to the
graves.

However, this does not mean that the concept of blessing
is minimal or insignificant. On the contrary, it remains a
dynamic force for the living. *Baraka* as blessing is an
element of Islam that seems well adapted to the traditional
African world view.

In discussing the concept of blessing in West Africa,
Trimingham (1959) distinguishes between theoretical Islam
and practical Islam. He says that in theoretical Islam there
is no longer any idea of holiness, as Islam has become rit-
ualized and secularized. This led, in the practical realm,
to the imbuement of the term *baraka* with relational qualities
of a link between God and man.

> The principle is relationship with the supernatural: the
> holy man is recognized as one near to God; the formula of
> the amulet is primarily the word of God, even though magi-
> cal formulas and symbols irreconcilable with Islam are
> used (p. 66).

In many parts of West Africa we would have to disagree
with Trimingham's conclusion that "it is surprising that the
idea of *baraka* has gained no essential hold on Negro Islam...
(that) the Muslim Negro has not adopted the word for the
mysterious forces he recognizes as everywhere present" (p. 66).
What he says may be true among "pure" Muslims in that they
reject that aspect of *baraka* which refers to a force peculiar
to certain persons and objects. But *baraka* as power remains
a vital part of Islam in West Africa, particularly among adherents of "popular" Islam.

As we study Islam in West Africa, we shall discover that
the culture of the people to which Islam came was, on the
one hand, changed by Islam, while on the other hand, the
culture itself changed Islam. Some of the Islamic brotherhoods became dynamic social and religious forces in West
Africa. We shall briefly explore the content of blessing in
two of these brotherhoods, one of which was particularly influenced by Islam in North Africa. We shall study blessing
in the lives of key figures in these Islamic orders.

The concept of blessing was viewed as a powerful force that
was particularly evident at certain points of transition in
one's life. The rites of passage were often laden with respect for and use of *baraka*. We shall describe the role of
blessing in key Islamic institutions and rites of passage.

Finally, we shall see that *baraka* is most commonly vis-
ualized in the life and ministry of Islamic religious leaders
(called clerics). The marabouts, *mallams*, and *moodibbos* of
West Africa to this day are respected and sought out by Muslims and non-Muslims alike because of this dynamic power in
their lives. We shall see that they struggle with syncretistic pressures and tendencies to mix religious dynamics of
blessing with animistic ones. This is particularly evident
in the rituals they perform.

BLESSING AND BROTHERHOODS IN WEST AFRICA

Several of the Islamic orders or brotherhoods which became prominent in North Africa also became significant in
West Africa. At the same time, some orders that became
significant in West Africa came directly from the Middle East.
Viewed by many as revitalization movements, using Wallace's
(1956) terminology, the impact of the brotherhoods was basically determined by the intensity and degree of charisma of
the leaders. Some brotherhoods leaned toward total militancy
while others were more moderate, emphasizing mysticism and
social reform in addition to *jihad* (holy war).

The two brotherhoods we shall briefly examine are the
Qadiriyya, the oldest of the brotherhoods which came from
the Middle East, led in West Africa by Usman dan Fodio, and
Tijaniyya, with its leading representative al-Hajj Umar Tal.
Both men possessed and exhibited a great deal of *baraka*.
They viewed blessing as a significant sign of God's direction,
calling, and empowering.

Usman dan Fodio and the Qadiriyya Order

Born in 1754 in the state of Gobir, Nigeria, Usman dan
Fodio grew up in the Torodbe clan of the Fulani tribe. This
clan was noted for its great emphasis on learning and piety.
The Torodbe were related to the cattle Fulani, but were mostly
settled.

Usman became a prolific writer and able scholar. He was
greatly influenced by the Malakite school of Islamic theology
with its strict observance of the Sunni interpretation of the
shari'a (law). But Usman was not only a Sunni. He also fell
heir to Sufistic influences. It was through the influence of
Jibril ibn 'Umar al-Aqdasi that Usman joined the Qadiriyya
order.

Jibril was greatly concerned with sin among his contempor-
aries. He was known as an outspoken preacher against anything anti-Islamic. Jibril was unquestionably the dominant
influence in Usman's life (Martin, 1976:18). Due to Jibril's
influence, Usman began preaching about reform and renewal at
the age of twenty. His fervent preaching and teaching attracted a great deal of attention and caused fear. He soon
had such a large following that some neighboring chiefs grew
edgy. For example, the chief of Gobir began to fear that his
throne was in danger. He thus issued orders that restricted
the spread of Islamic teaching.

As the leader of the Qadiriyya order in this part of West
Africa, Usman often withdrew to the desert or other secluded
places to meditate and perform the Sufi litanies. It was
during times of meditation that he claimed to have experienced,
through visions, contact with Sheikh Abol al-Qadiri, the
founder of the order in the 13th century. Usman saw that his
silsila (chain of blessing) was through al-Qadiri. It was
thus through this Sufi order that Usman laid claim to *baraka*,
the blessing of God. With the assurance that God was blessing him, he felt the call to become a reformer and reviver
of Islam (*mujaddid al-Islam*).

His acts as reformer were non-militant at first. His
tactics were preaching and teaching. The main subjects of
his sermons were the unity of God, the foundations of faith,
righteousness, sin and punishment, paradise and eternal happiness (Johnston, 1967:36). The more he preached and taught
as he traveled through the area, the greater became his fame.
He received the title of Shehu (from *sheikh* in Arabic) and
was viewed by most people as a man of great blessing.

Both Hausas and Fulahs believe that the founder of the
empire, Dan Fodio, possessed supernatural power, that he
ranks next after Christ, and that his power of blessing
or banning has descended on his successors (Wallace, 1896:
217).

While this assessment may be based more on enthusiastic devotion than on facts, it indicates the intensity of the impact
that Usman had on people.

Later on, the Shehu became more and more angered by the
laxness of the Muslim community in living its faith. He began to vehemently detest nominality. Along with his religious fervor there developed a simultaneous political enmity
with the local chief. After an attempt on his life failed,

Usman fled for refuge, an event which he compared to the Prophet's fleeing from Mecca to Medina.

When the local chief, Yunfa, declared war, the die was cast. The Fulani Muslims looked to their charismatic leader Usman dan Fodio for guidance. Muhammadu Bello, his son, and later first sultan of the Sokoto Empire, describes the scene in his writing *Infaku'l Maisuri*.

At this we gathered together and took stock of our affairs. We decided that it was not right for men to be leaderless, without a chief, so then and there we paid homage to Shehu. We promised to obey his commands and to follow him alike in prosperity and adversity. He accepted our allegiance and himself vowed to follow the Book and the Law (Arnett, 1922:51).

The result was the famous Fulani *jihad* which has become brilliant military and religious history. Inspired by the dual purposes of removing *habe* (pagan) misrule and reforming the Islamic way of life, the *jihad* touched not only moral behavior, but also political institutions and the system of the *shari'a* (law).

Through the *jihad*, Shehu Usman dan Fodio's claim to *baraka* became recognized as valid. Because of his charismatic leadership, his influence has had a lasting effect on the people of northern Nigeria and neighboring countries. Their continual homage to him is vividly seen in the pilgrimages many Muslims make to his tomb.

Even though there is not a great deal of veneration of saints' tombs in West Africa, the shrine of Usman dan Fodio is an exception. The author remembers several Fulanis in Cameroon who claimed to have received great blessing from making a pilgrimage to Yola and then to Usman's tomb at Sokoto. "Like the marabout of North-west Africa, Usmaanu is the wellspring of blessing" (Martenson, 1977:124).

We see an example of this homage in the words of blessing of Tamus Bamu Allah Almakha Aldaya, author of *Sawaabu Seehu Usmaanu*.

I thank you, Seehu, blessed apostle of God
For the answers to my prayers to God!
O honorable Seehu, lord of glory,
You are shown how to take care of the needs of the saints...

O Seehu, your glory
Fills all the countries with your blessing
Beloved one, believers find contentment in your name
You have lifted up, exalted and honored their glory...

Because of your blessing Seehu your land is full of
        possessions
Both East and West are full of the believer's riches
Because of that blessing they are your heirs...

O honored Usmaanu because of your blessing
Draw me and fill me with your gifts
Cause me to drink from your source the river of science
I too will be among those that have their thirst satisfied.
                                (Martenson, 1977:148-58)

Even though the Qadiriyya order has lost influence in
West Africa in the twentieth century, the homage paid to Usman continues to be impressive. For example, even though the
conversion of Emir Abbas in the early part of the 20th century to the Tijaniyya order "resulted in a substantial reorientation of the Fulani mallam class from Qadiriyya to
Tijaniyya," (Paden, 1973:73), the praise of Usman has not
been significantly affected.

Al-Hajj Umar Tal and the Tijaniyya Order

The aim of all Islamic reformers and their orders was to
return the practices of Muslims to the pristine concept of
Islam as based on the Qur'an and as conceived and interpreted
by the brotherhood. They also hoped to Islamize the whole
area under their influence. As we have seen, this objective
has often resulted in multi-level strategies, including
social and spiritual reform. In addition, it usually involved military maneuvers.

While Usman dan Fodio used the holy war to attain his goal,
he and his order had a high mystical priority of bringing
people to faith in God by an intensive missionary approach.
But, when we come to another Islamic reformer, al-Hajj Umar
Tal, we find quite a different story. His approach was primarily a militant one, though he claimed allegiance to mysticism.

Al-Hajj Umar Tal (1794-1864) was, like Usman dan Fodio, a
member of the Torodbe clan of Fulanis. But growing up in
northern Senegal, his contacts with Sufi brotherhoods were
different. He was an intellectual and became attracted to

mysticism early in life. As a young adult, he met representatives of the Tijaniyya order of Sufis. Tijaniyya was a
reforming order that was stricter than the Qadiriyya order.
It "preached a more egalitarian Islam, which allowed a greater number to accede to the *baraka*" (Tapiero, 1969:65).

After an extended pilgrimage to Mecca, where he was named
caliph of Western Africa for the Tijaniyya order, he returned
to carry out his mandate. He spent several years in the Sokoto Empire, befriending Muhammadu Bello, the sultan. Even
though Bello was a member of the Qadiriyya order, he accepted
Umar and gave him a daughter to marry.

Umar later returned to his home and set out to Islamize
the area west of Masina (present day eastern Senegal and
northern Upper Volta). His strategy was strictly militaristic. Because of insatiable lust for conquest, he "lapsed
from spiritual leadership, but used Tijani allegiance to bind
his Tukolor followers to himself as *khalifa*" (Trimingham,
1968:16). His followers devoted themselves to the *baraka* of
the order and of their leader and bound themselves to the
cause of the *jihad*. This decision naturally involved widespread conflict with other Muslims, with non-Muslims, and with
the colonizing French government. But commitment to Umar and
the Tijanniya order meant total domination or nothing at all
(Lewis, 1966:78).

As Umar expanded his conquest of the western Sahel, he
imposed Tijaniyya allegiance as the official religious cult.
He had earlier written a commentary on the theology of the
Tijaniyya order. The *Rimah* has remained a source of blessing
and guidance for Tijanis to the present day. But his victor-
ious expansion resulted in overconfidence. This, in turn,
led him to a fatal trap. He did not believe that his enemies
would be able to mobilize and form a large coalition against
him. When they did, he found himself unable to escape. Reli-
able oral traditions say that Umar committed suicide by blow-
ing himself up with gun powder (Martin, 1976:98).

While the impact of blessing in the life and continuing
influence of Umar was not nearly as great as that of Usman
dan Fodio, his far-reaching conquest and Islamization has had
a deep effect on the status of Islam in West Africa. Today,
it is the Tijaniyya order that is the most influential in West
Africa. Its liturgical litanies and rituals continue to
bring blessing to its numerous adherents.

The impact of *baraka* in the religious orders is different
in several ways in West Africa than in North Africa. Yet
it has played just as significant a role in the development
and spread of Islam. The religious orders have been a "factor in the interchange of men and ideas, and have opened the
way for a few to enter into a dimension of Islam deeper than
the legalism which tends to predominate Negro territory by
their stress on ethical aspects" (Trimingham, 1968:77).

BLESSING AND RITES OF PASSAGE

The impact of the *jihad* and the Islamic reforms of Usman
dan Fodio and other reformers can still be seen in West Africa today. Whether a tribe be truly Muslim or only nominally
Muslim, Islamic rites are almost always followed. As is
true among Muslims everywhere, the dynamic role of blessing
is an integral part of these transition rituals. We shall
examine three of these rites of passage: birth and name
giving, circumcision, and marriage. Our references will be
primarily from Cameroon and Nigeria.

Birth and Name Giving

As in North Africa, the pregnant Muslim woman of West
Africa is viewed as possessing *baraka*. Fertility is a vital
aspect of blessing in Islam as it is in the biblical record.
When a woman is discovered to be pregnant, she is treated as
a special person. There is great fear that the blessing of
her pregnancy might be polluted. Because of this, a nomadic
pregnant Fulani woman often remains alone in a special place
called a *suura*. She must avoid all contacts with men, even
her husband. Contact with cattle can also "spoil" the blessing of her pregnancy.

When birth occurs, an interesting phenomenon takes place.
The *baraka* of the woman passes to the child. She loses her
baraka and is viewed as unclean. For a period of time, as
when she has her menstrual period, she is not allowed to enter the mosque or place of prayer.

The first child of Fulanis is called *afo* and is especially
blessed. Twins are also viewed as a sign of God's blessing
and favor. This is radically different from some animistic
tribes (Tchamba in Northern Cameroon, for instance) where
twins are believed to bring a curse on the village. These
twins are usually killed by drowning unless some Fulanis or
other tribespeople are willing to adopt them and remove them
from the village.

Baraka is conferred at the birth of a child in a special
ritual performed by the Muslim *mallam* (holy man, teacher).
Upon hearing of the birth of a child, he will come and whis-
per the *shahada* (creed) and other Islamic prayers in the
child's ear.   In this way he blesses the child with God's
word and witness to the Islamic faith.

Seven days after the birth, the naming ceremony occurs.
Again among Fulanis, it is the *mallam* who has the responsibility of choosing the name of the child.   It is a time of
great celebration with friends and relatives coming to participate in the ritual and festival of blessing.   The name
is carefully chosen because the name carries with it deep
meaning and blessing.   The first name a child receives in his
life is this religious one by the *mallam*.   For male children
the *mallam* will choose one of the names by which the Prophet
was known, such as Muhammad, Mahmud, Hamid, or Mustafa, or
one of the ninety-nine variants by which God is addressed.
For females one of the names of the women in the Prophet's
family is normally given: Khadijah, Fatimah, A'ishah, or
Zaynab (Farah, 1968:167).   A child is not regarded as a real
person until the name giving ceremony is completed.   At a
later date (although sometimes it occurs at the name giving
ceremony) the child may be given a private, personal name,
a grandparent's name, a nickname, or even an adopted name.

The Fulani name giving ceremony (*inndere*) is essentially
the same as the Arabic *'aqiqa*.   The Islamic canon law requires that the child's head be shaved and that an animal be
sacrificed.   Some of the meat is eaten by the family of the
child, but most of it is given as alms to the poor.   The pastoral Fulani describe the Islamic basis for the name giving
ceremony with the words: "The child should sleep for a week,
we should make a name-feast, we should sacrifice--thus the
Book says" (Stenning, 1959:117-18).

Circumcision

A second rite of passage charged with *baraka* is circumcision.   Even though circumcision is not found in the Qur'an,
it has become a significant event in the life of the Muslim
male.   While some "schools" of Islam view circumcision as
indispensable, others regard it as only commendable.   Yet, it
is commonly viewed as one of the most important rites in Islam (Levy, 1957:251).

Theologically, circumcision is presented as part of the
purification process necessary before proper prayer can be

made. Realistically, it is, along with the *shahada*, required
for one to become a Muslim in West Africa. The Fulani word
for circumcision is *juulnol*. The word for Muslim is *juuldo*.
Thus we see that circumcision and becoming a Muslim are inseparable.

Unlike many other African societies, circumcision in Islam
is not particularly associated with any rite of initiation
(Trimingham, 1968:70). It is primarily an individual rite,
a ceremony of purification. It may have social elements if
it is performed at or near the age of puberty. This may
happen when an animistic tribe becomes Muslim but retains
many of its former customs. Circumcision may then become
initiation into manhood. But normally Islam has the aim and
effect of desacralizing animistic circumcision so that it is
reduced to a simple Islamic rite. West African Muslims circumcise at various ages, some seven days or forty days after
birth, others (though rarely) even after puberty. The most
common age, however, is seven to ten years.

Baraka is a prevalent part of circumcision in its cultic
aspects. The reading and memorizing of the Qur'an or certain
Qur'anic passages brings the blessings of the holy word and
language. In Songhay the Muslim clerics chant the Qur'an
into sand which is scattered on the floor of the circumcision
hut to expel and protect against spirits during this critical
period (Trimingham, 1968:71).

The sanctity of circumcision is often guarded by the giving of *sadaka* (sacrificial offering). This is theologically
related to the Abrahamic story where the blessing of sacrifice is connected to circumcision which became the symbol of
covenant. Therefore, Muslims circumcise because God ordained
it as a holy act, not because it was a custom of the ancestors. As such, it is an act of blessing for the individual,
one which opens the door for him to faith. Circumcision becomes initiation into the community of Islam.

Marriage

The impact of blessing is also evident in marriage relationships. Because marriage customs and rules vary consider-
ably in different societies according to the tenacity of the
custom and the strength of Islamic pressure towards change,
our brief treatment of blessing in marriage will be general
in scope. Yet, it remains a vital aspect of Muslim's understanding of the marriage ceremony and relationship.

In most Muslim weddings, *baraka* is ascribed to the bride
and groom. There seems to be something "supernatural" about
the event as the couple starts a new life and enters into the
mysteries of marriage and its functions. While most West
Africans do not postulate marriage as a factor in determining
one's eternal destiny, like they do in many parts of Morocco,
they do view it as a ritual and event that is sanctioned and
blessed by God.

Islamic marriage is distinguished from typical animistic
African marriages in that it is a contract or arrangement between two individuals, not between two families. A Muslim
cleric performs the marriage ceremony which is appropriately
solemnized by witnesses. Actually, there are a series of
ceremonies, commencing with betrothal ceremonies and ending
with the consummation wedding ceremony. The essential feature of the marriage ritual is the "declaration and the acceptance." The *mallam* announces the acceptance of the agreement (the bride and groom and their fathers are usually not
present--they have sent friends as representatives), recites
a formula which binds the contract, and then leads in the
recital of the *fatihah* (the opening chapter of the Qur'an)
and the *salat 'ala'n-nabi*. He will also pray for good health,
children, and wealth for the new couple. Thus we see that it
is the holy word and prayer that blesses the marriage trans-
action.

Another indication in Islamic marriage of the role of *baraka* is in the general insistence of Islam on virginity. The
bride must come to her groom as holy, untouched. Most Muslim
ceremonies include "defloration as part of the rite, and exhibit the 'signs of virginity'" (Trimingham, 1959:173).

We have thus seen that the dynamic role of blessing is a
crucial element in the key rites of passage of the living.
Its presence is assured by the participation of the religious
clerics. It is proclaimed both through the spoken word and
ritual acts. However, the Muslim cleric participates in the
realm of blessing in other ways as well, as we shall see next.

BLESSING AND MUSLIM CLERICS

As one studies the process by which animists become Muslims, one sees that religious leaders play a significant role.
While it is incorrect to assert that in Islam there is an
"ordained" clergy, a sacerdotal body, there does exist a hier-
archy of religious roles of sorts whose functions are performed by men with a vast range of abilities and education.

They range from the uneducated *mallam* or *moodibbo* to the
marabout and *imam*.

Muslim clerics played a significant role in the process
of religious and cultural change that took place as Islam
made and continues to make inroads into animistic Africa.
Instead of an adaptation of Islam to Africa, the process has
been one of accommodation or acculturation of Islamic customs.
The strategy and role of the clerics was to get "certain min-
imum Islamic requirements accepted into the body of custom...
The result is a fusion in life but not a true synthesis"
(Trimingham, 1968:46).

As Islamic customs became a more basic part of African
life, the clerics attempted to redirect the devotion to and
care of ancestral community toward the worship of God. In
this process there was a great struggle with the tendencies
to syncretize the old and the new. Because Islam as a religion touches every aspect of the individual's life and
merges them into one, the process of religious change has
been an enormous one. We have already seen some of the ways
in which the clerics acculturated Islam into the rites of
passage which were so basic to animistic life.

The process of religious change is a continuing one. Thus
the role of Muslim clerics is three-fold: to continue participating in the process of conversion from animism (sometimes also from Christianity) to Islam, to instruct and
deepen the faith, commitment, and understanding of Muslims,
and to meet the felt-needs of the people. The goal is to
develop an Islamic community that is distinguishable from
others by its outward worship of God and by a consistency
of character and conduct. The cleric is the religious leader
of this community because of his closeness to God through the
baraka he has received.

We can divide the religious tasks, roles, and functions of
Muslim clerics into three major categories. They are teacher
and preacher, liturgist, and healer. Because they are not
usually salaried (they do receive gifts for their services),
most Muslim clerics also have other occupations such as com-
merce and farming. Yet they retain the distinction of being
a class of learned specialists.

The Muslim Cleric as Teacher and Preacher

Among most Muslim peoples today, a significant gap exists
between men and women and between the learned and the un-

learned. Although this gap is being narrowed somewhat in
urban centers in West Africa where the effects of moderniza-
tion are felt the greatest, it still remains an essential
feature of Islam. The gap is assured to an extent by the
emphasis Islam places on the ability to study and learn.
Through Qur'anic schools, certain students excel in their
ability to recite the Qur'an and to explain the tenets of
Islam. This ability places them in a class of learned specialists which accompanies the spread of Islam everywhere
(Greenberg, 1946:65).

One becomes a religious teacher or preacher through an
apprenticeship program. It is much like a master-disciple
relationship. The student lives with his master and assists
with the work of the *mallam* (comes from *mu'allim* in Arabic,
meaning teacher). As he grows in stature in the larger Islamic community, the student becomes himself a *mallam* and
may become attached to a governmental official. With such
status usually he will be designated a marabout or even *imam*.
If his position includes meting out justice at a higher level,
he will be called *alkaali*.

The ideal aim of all Muslims is to be a scholar. Through
being well-versed in the Qur'an, the *Hadith* (the traditions),
and Islamic theology, such a master will discover the true
piety which teaching brings.

The function of preaching is usually done by the Muslim
cleric in larger mosques on Friday, the day of worship. It
is called a "Qur'anic interpretation session." To begin the
session, a worshiper recites a passage of the Qur'an he has
memorized. Then the cleric will repeat it and comment on it
and its meaning. There may also be a homily or sermon.

The Muslim Cleric as Liturgist

As the religious leader of a small village or large city,
the Muslim cleric has numerous and specific liturgical functions. In addition to those we have already discussed,
birth and name giving, circumcision, and marriage, the cleric
also washes the dead and conducts the funeral prayers. He
leads in prayers at worship and directs the observance of the
pillars of faith.

Although the sphere of his influence may be proportional
to his *baraka*, the Muslim cleric is viewed as a holy man.
This gives him the right and responsibility of leading in all
aspects of religious life. Because prayer is the principle

duty of all Muslims, the presence and impact of the cleric is
most evident in the worship of God. If the place of prayer
(mosque) is a small one, the cleric may be the only one in
the open area while the rest of the worshipers arrange themselves behind him.

In Islam the ritual of worship is fixed and rigid. Every
detail is established for ritual prayer. "Strict clerics
claim that variation renders prayer invalid" (Trimingham,
1959:71). Because of this rigidity, the nominal Muslim is
often content to let the cleric do the ritual prayers for
him. A true Muslim prays at least five times a day. As
religious leader, the cleric strictly follows this require-
ment. For those who are less faithful, he becomes a mediator,
praying in their place. However, there are informal prayers
which any Muslim can pray any time and any place which do
not require strict observances of ritual.

An additional function of the Muslim cleric is serving as
head sacrificer. During special religious festivals, such
as the Festival of the Sheep, the cleric will be the one to
cut the first sheep's throat, making sure the animal is facing toward Mecca, and that all other ritual customs are
followed. In performing these and other sacrificial functions, the cleric is called *liman* (priest). Where there has
been a large degree of syncretism with animism, the Muslim
liman often replaces the animistic priest in performing agri-
cultural rituals and propitiating the spirits.

All the liturgical functions that a Muslim cleric performs
are viewed as functions of blessing from God. It is the
effective acts of the cleric which help bring the worshiper
closer to God.

The Muslim Cleric as Healer

The function of healing is a controversial one in West
African Islam. Because the process of healing often involves the use of charms and amulets, and the drinking of
"divine liquid," many orthodox and modern Muslims do not
consider West African clerics to be valid Muslims. These
orthodox Muslims are not willing to accept elements and
divination they perceive to be magical as true and faithful
to the Qur'an and to Islam.

In spite of this rejection, one finds the making of amulets and "divine liquids" a widespread phenomenon in West
Africa. Here it is believed that the Muslim cleric has the

ability to bring the power of God (*baraka*) to a person's life through ritual words, actions, and objects.

In the amulet, it is the power of the sacred Arabic language that is believed to bestow *baraka*. The Muslim cleric is believed to have inherited God's blessing and thus has the ability to confer this power through the amulet. It is at this point that Islam faces the issue of syncretistic magic and true religion. The use of amulets is permitted by many Muslims because Islamic amulets involve prayer to God as well as magical knowledge. Trimingham (1959) states:

> To the wearer the amulet is magical in operation, but religious in drawing on the power of the name of God and His angels. The cleric therefore performs his magical functions within the domain of Islam, and his attitude to magic is based, not on the end, but the method employed (p. 112-13).

In spite of modern and orthodox Islamic rejection of magical elements as a valid aspect of Islam, many Orthodox Muslims have these amulets on their horses and in their homes. When the author asked about the use or possession of these amulets, an orthodox Muslim replied that they were simply decorations.

In addition to a wide assortment of amulets, each claiming a special function or type of protection, West African clerics also serve as healers of the ill. A commonly used method of healing is the writing of Arabic phrases (usually claimed to be from the Qur'an) on a wooden board. These holy words are then washed off with water and the solution is collected in a cup and given to the sick person. This "divine liquid" solution is believed to contain *baraka* to cure the illness. The author's Fulani language informant in Cameroon was a cleric who received a good portion of his income through this healing ministry. He claimed that it was the *baraka* of the holy language that carried within it healing power.

As healer, the Muslim cleric may also use divination. Through the manipulation of sand, the Qur'an, numbers, or rosaries, the cleric is said to be able to discover sources of illness or evil. There is also great use of dreams, ordeals, spirit possession, and necromancy. It is believed through these methods that what they say, do, and discover is directed and blessed by God. As related previously, dreams were used by Fulani leaders such as Usman dan Fodio to receive guidance and conviction before making decisions.

A significant characteristic of the life of Muslim clerics
and Islam is mobility. Only in urban centers is the mosque
a permanent building. In rural areas the mosque may be an
open space marked by sticks or surrounded by a grass woven
fence. The Muslim cleric is often mobile, traveling from
one area to another. One can come across "wandering friars
with, clung around them, a goatskin or mat *sijjada*, ablution
jug, bookbag, and pencase" (Trimingham, 1968:60).

Perhaps this mobility is one reason why Islam has encountered animism throughout West Africa. It is in the func-
ions of the Muslim clerics that one observes syncretistic
tendencies and struggles within Islam. Believing that bestowing the blessing of God is part of their responsibility,
they have often found it difficult to distinguish clearly
between God's true power of blessing and animistic powers.
It is easy for the two religions to become mixed at this
point.

Froelich (1962:134) gives an example of this ease of syncretism. In the 18th century a Malinke Muslim returned
from the pilgrimage to Mecca carrying a Qur'an in a straw
basket filled with sand from the holy city. He kept the
basket in his home village. However, over a period of time,
the article became an animistic fetish. People began to
sacrifice chickens near it, dropping the blood on the basket
and its contents. In 1918 an orthodox Muslim discovered
that the book was indeed the Qur'an and squelched the practice.

This is only one of many instances where an Islamic holy
article has become an animistic fetish or idol. It indicates
the danger of syncretism occurring when religious or supernatural values are attached to articles or objects.

Gilliland (1971) describes the interaction of and tension
between Islam and animism on this issue:

Extreme pressure is put on both religions to neutralize
existential problems... The means of maintaining balance
and providing options for the society are provided by
different levels of functionaries who, whether Muslim or
traditional, find it to their disadvantage to work in a
mutually exclusive way (p. 209-10).

One often discovers animists who, not finding help from
their traditional priests or diviners, go to a Muslim cleric
to seek the aid they need. On the other hand, they believe
that there are some areas of knowledge that a Muslim cleric

knows nothing about. This indicates a distinct bifurcation
of the roles of the clerics in animism and Islam.

Summary

In this section we have seen that the dynamic role of blessing is a significant force in the world of Islam. Not only
is it a Qur'anic concept, but both popular and orthodox Muslims deem it a vital part of God's relationship with people.
However, this does not eliminate controversy over the concept
and its use.

We see in the development of Sufistic mysticism that blessing (*baraka*) became a highly sought power. The whole phenomenon of the veneration of saints is based on the existence
and influence of this pervasive force. In both North and
West Africa *baraka* is believed to be fundamental to one's
faith and religious practice. While the power of *baraka* is
sometimes used in questionable ways, such as magical methods
of healing, its misuse does not negate or reduce the impact
it has had and continues to have on Islamic life and outreach
in Africa today. Its influence touches people at every
significant transition point and moment of crisis in their
lives.

In West Africa the power of blessing is basic to the ministry of Islamic religious leaders. It permits them to minister to the needs of people through words and actions. One
discovers blessing in action at all levels of society.

Linguistically, *baraka* is most often an expression of
praise and blessing. The word, or one of its forms, is used
to bless others, especially in greeting one in a superior
position, such as the chief. In a personal letter to the

author (1978), Dr. Leslie Stennes verified its wide use among
Fulanis from Cameroon to Upper Volta. In addition to blessing, *baraka* sometimes carries the connotation of grace, mercy,
and thanksgiving.

The concept of blessing is thus an important one in Islamic society in both North and West Africa. Because of its
close relationship in meaning to its biblical counterparts,
it is a natural redemptive analogy for the Church in its
witness, especially in Islamic West Africa.

The question now facing us is: What is the relationship
of blessing as understood and used by Muslims to that of the
Church and the Bible? Is the concept of blessing in the Bible and the life of the Church of significant proportion that
it can serve as an effective link in building bridges to
Muslims, particularly in Africa? In the next section we
shall explore blessing in the Bible and the life of the
Church, studying its potential for increasing the effectiveness of mission to Muslims in Africa.

III

Blessing in the Bible and the Church

If one were to ask the question, "What is the Bible all about?" a brief but fair answer would be, "An account of God's divine action with man and man's interaction with God." The basic message of both Old and New Testaments is that God relates to people.

In the annals of the Old Testament we find the story of the acts of God, first in creation and then in the history of his chosen people. The New Testament highlights the deliverance and salvation of people by God in Jesus Christ as its central motif.

The story of God as creator is the overture to the ongoing drama of his action in the world. God spoke strong rhythmic words and the universe came into being. It was full of majesty and beauty. But then the scene changed and it became darkened by man's rebellion and sin. Chaos replaced peace and harmony, self-aggrandisement took the place of humility.

Because of this disastrous event, the account shifts from the acts of God in creation to the saving acts of God in history, the history of the people of Israel. Primeval history becomes family history as God begins to work out his saving acts. Salvation and covenant become key themes. Leaders such as Abraham and Moses respond in faith. The Pentateuch develops the account of the people's confession of faith and praise to God for his mighty acts of love and deliverance.

But there remains another key facet of God's action in
history. It is a different kind of action. It is not a
momentary act such as deliverance. It is, instead, an ongoing act. It is God's divine work of blessing. It becomes
God's way of empowering and encouraging his people. "When
the Bible speaks of God's contact with mankind, his blessing
is there alongside his deliverance. History comes into being
only when both are there together" (Westermann, 1978:4).

We discover in the New Testament that God, in bringing
salvation, did not deliver his people only *from* slavery and
sin; he also delivered them *to* a new life, a new state of
blessing that was designed for growth, prosperity, enrichment,
and maturity.

From the beginning of the Old Testament to the end of the
New Testament these two aspects--deliverance and blessing--
are found together. They are both part of God's activity in
the world. We cannot have one without the other. Yet we
must carefully distinguish between them.

They cannot be reduced to a single concept because, for
one reason, they are experienced differently. Deliverance
is experienced in events that represent God's intervention.
Blessing is a continuing activity of God that is either
present or not present (Westermann, 1978:4).

Blessing occurs in the recorded words of Jesus, is attested
to by most New Testament writers, and played significant
roles in the ministry and mission of the early Church. Clearly, the picture is incomplete if the concept of blessing is
disregarded or missing in one's Christology, ecclesiology,
and missiology.

5

The Source and Content of Blessing

The concept of blessing, which is so important in the Islamic world, is equally significant in the Bible. Blessing was seen by the people of God as having its source in God. He is the Source of Sources. Blessing is something which is dependent on God who himself alone can give it or withhold it (Weiser, 1962;87).

GOD AS THE SOURCE AND GIVER OF BLESSING

In the Old Testament we see that when God commanded Abraham to leave his country and family and go to a new land (Gen. 12), the wording is clear and unmistakable in its emphasis on the divine intention behind the command. Abraham was to be a blessing; he would become God's divine gift to the world. He was to be a blessing, not just receive a blessing.

The blessing is, therefore, a sacred act, a holy gift bestowed on man by God. Abraham became a recipient and bearer of a divine promise and power. He would become an instrument, a communicator of blessing which he had received from God through faith. Blessing became a significant aspect of his life. Abraham's life and personality had no special significance apart from his faith and the blessing it brought from God. This divine act of God set Abraham immediately on the road to mission. "The call of Abraham from the beginning concerned others as well as himself and his immediate descendants. Every facet of the blessing implies a mission" (Milton, 1961:52).

When a man, like Abraham, receives a blessing from God, he receives the power inherent in blessing. In turn, that power becomes his power and he becomes a source and transmitter of that power to others. To be blessed means to have a part in God's divine power and to be able to share this power with others (Van den Doel, 1968:37). But Abraham never claims to become the ultimate source of this power. He always acknowledges God as the original source, the primary giver of blessing.

As the source and genesis of blessing, God chose to give this power to those who were open and obedient to him. Obedience is a crucial part of blessing because a man is blessed not only when God has done something for him, but when, through obedience, he is able to do something for others. Particularly from the time of the Sinaitic covenant, the Old Testament is clear in its assertion that the reception of blessing required obedience. If obedience was missing, the blessing would become a curse. There is no stronger warning than Mal. 2:2 where the prophet says, "If you will not listen, if you will not lay it to your heart to give glory to my name, says the Lord of Hosts, then I will send the curse upon you and I will curse your blessings; indeed I have already cursed them, because you do not lay it to heart."

Thus, the emphasis in the Old Testament is on blessing as a holistic power working in the lives of his chosen, obedient servants. Abraham as the first of the patriarchs is one (but a key one) of many such blessed people. Because they represent God, they are gifted with the power to bless others. This is particularly true of the king, the priest, and the seer or prophet.

The New Testament confirms and reaffirms the fact that God is the source of blessing. However, in the New Testament we see a transformation of some aspects of blessing.

There are eight passages in the New Testament which speak of God as the source and giver of blessing. In 1 Pet. 3:9; Heb. 6:7-8, 12-15, and Matt. 25:34, we discover a common theme: man inheriting the blessing given by God. The passages in the book of Hebrews have, as their starting point, the patriarchal blessings. The blessing of Abraham became the center of the covenant between God and his people. The author of Hebrews sees the blessing of the patriarchs by God as having significance "in that they foretell the replacing of the Jews by the Christians as the Sons of the covenant" (Van den Doel, 1968:148).

The author of Hebrews is retelling the facts of the Old
Testament covenant of blessing so that the Christian Church
could understand its role as that of inheritor of God's
blessing. The Church is to be like Abraham, "so that you may
not be sluggish, but imitators of those who through faith and
patience inherit the promises" (Heb. 6:12). "And thus Abraham, having patiently endured, obtained (inherited) the promise" (Heb. 6:15). The writer refers again to elements of
the promise, such as land and seed: "For the land which has
drunk the rain that often falls upon it and brings forth
vegetation useful to those for whose sake it is cultivated,
receives a blessing from God" (Heb. 6:7-8).

As faith was a strategic and crucial element for Abraham
in receiving the blessing, so it is for the Church. It is
the starting point for believers. It is faith that ushers
the individual into the saving relationship with God. Through
that faith God also begins to pour out his blessings on the
believer, and corporately, on the congregation of believers.
In this way the Church inherits the blessing as did the
patriarchs.

1 Pet. 3:9 also describes the reception of God's blessing
in terms of inheritance. The fact that the three verses
following verse nine are a quote from Ps. 34:12-16 indicates
that Peter, in proclaiming the blessing of God, is using
terminology that is based on an Old Testament understanding
of blessing.

The passage from Matt. 25:34, "Come, O blessed of my Father, inherit the kingdom prepared for you from the foundation of the world," is a description of salvation using the
language of blessing. Based on Isa. 65:23, which describes
the consummation of salvation--the people will be called the
"offspring of the blessed of the Lord"--it seems to refer to
the fulfillment of the prophetic "portrayal of a future state
of salvation" (Westermann, 1978:81).

These passages indicate a strong reliance on and use of
the Old Testament understanding of blessing. But they point
to the Church as the inheritor of the ultimate blessing which
was Christ and the salvation he brought.

Acts 3:25-26, Gal. 3:8-9,14, and Eph. 1:3, in speaking of
God's blessings, also refer to the patriarchs, especially
Abraham. But they are different in that they transform the
blessings from patriarchal to Christological. All refer to
the relationship between the promise of blessing given to

Abraham and the fulfillment of that promise in Christ. God's
saving act in Christ is called a blessing because of the promise of blessing given to the patriarchs.

Acts 3:25-26 and Gal. 3:8-9,14 specifically declare that
the promise to Abraham is completed in Christ. Westermann
(1978) calls this transformation the "Christianization of the
concept of blessing" (p. 77). In these verses blessing becomes a synonym for God's saving action in Christ. Schenk
(1967) comes to the same conclusion when he states, "As in
Gal. 3, so is it also here (Acts 3:25) that Christ is viewed
as the fulfillment in salvation history of the promise to
Abraham, (he is) the fulfillment of blessing" (p. 47).

While the remaining passage, Eph. 1:3, uses somewhat different language, its emphasis is the same; that in Christ the
believer inherits the ultimate blessing of God. The "spiritual blessing in Christ" is the redemptive work of God. In
this introduction of praise, Paul is asserting that God's
work of salvation in Christ is his crown of blessing. "Blessing is thus understood entirely in Christological or soteriological terms" (Westermann, 1978:79).

Thus, we see in these eight passages that the New Testament
retains the emphasis of the Old Testament which holds that
God is seen as performing primarily redemptive acts. There
are several references to material blessings, but the spiritual blessing God gives through faith in the risen Christ does
receive a greater emphasis. However, the New Testament is
careful to emphasize the holistic impact of blessing, material and spiritual.

JESUS AS THE SOURCE AND GIVER OF BLESSING

While God is the acknowledged source of all blessings, the
New Testament reveals Jesus as having a major role in blessing. The Gospels report Jesus as blessing people both before
and after his resurrection. We can divide the times when
Jesus blessed people into three categories. These categories
are: blessing the children, blessing food before eating, and
blessing his disciples before his ascension.

Jesus Blesses Children

Each of the Synoptic Gospels records the event of Jesus
blessing the children. While only Mark (the earliest Gospel)
uses the word "bless," the other two mean exactly the same
thing when they say "lay his hands on them and pray" (Matt.

19:13) and "he should touch them" (Luke 18:15). While the
blessing of children by the father, and later by the rabbi
during festivals such as the Day of Atonement, was customary,
the blessing of children by Jesus is given new meaning.
He does this by relating the blessing of the children to the
Kingdom of God. The blessing becomes an entrance into the
Kingdom. Brun (1932) sees this transformation in the meaning
of blessing when he states, "...Jesus' words of blessing and
his laying his hands on the children's heads had a direct
effect that lasted beyond the moment... His blessing and
the laying on of hands impart to the children in some way the
Kingdom itself" (p. 20).

Jesus Blesses Meals

On another occasion when Jesus becomes the blesser, he is
eating a meal with his disciples. Again he follows the custom of the Jews in blessing the food. Upon receiving the
food which is the fruit of the fields that has grown by the
power of God's blessing, Jesus gives thanks to God. But this
act of blessing becomes more than a customary act. In the
feeding of the multitude (Luke 9:10-17, Matt. 15:29-38), the
blessing becomes the initiatory part of a miraculous event.
At the Last Supper in the upper room (Matt. 26, Luke 22), Jesus blesses the bread and wine. However, he then ties in the
blessing of the two elements with his death and the eternal
significance of redemption for his followers. His post-resur-
rection meal at Emmaus (Luke 24:28-31) indicates only the
traditional custom of blessing food. However, the impact
of the total event had an intense effect on the two men:
"Did not our hearts burn within us!"

Jesus Blesses His Disciples

Jesus' final act of blessing took place on a hill near
Bethany. He lifted his hands over his disciples and blessed
them as he ascended into the heavens. At first glance, this
seems to be a customary blessing of departure. No doubt this
custom was the framework of the blessing. But the words that
Jesus spoke and the context in which they were spoken indicate
that the words of blessing were more than just a farewell
statement. In Acts 1 Luke reveals the important relationship
between Jesus' farewell blessing and the empowering of the
Holy Spirit. Christ was not taking the power of blessing
with him to heaven. Instead, he leaves it with his disciples
and his Church. His blessing was to continue in the life and
ministry of the Church as it was empowered by the Holy Spirit.

In reviewing these three types of blessing by Jesus, we
see he uses traditional forms and common customs. But
through these normal forms and customs Jesus introduces new
meanings. In each event of blessing we see the power of God.
Each blessing is identified with an act that represents the
redemptive and empowering word of God. In the laying of hands
on the children, blessing is "connected with the entering of
the Kingdom, in the blessing of the bread with the memorial
meal, and in the parting blessing with the glorification of
the Son of God" (Westermann, 1978:30).

In summary then, we see that in all the references where
Jesus is the source and giver of blessing, he takes over the
Old Testament understanding and form of blessing and through
it introduces its relationship to the Kingdom of God and the
life of the Church. Blessing in the Church means a continuity
in the life of the congregation; it means the people of God
are guided and empowered by the Holy Spirit so there is
growth, strengthening, and maturation. Yet, at the same time,
we must understand the close relationship of blessing to,
but not complete identification with or absorption into,
salvation. In each case where Jesus is the blesser, "the
blessing is subordinated to a saving act of Christ but not
absorbed into it" (Westermann, 1978:100).

THE CONTENT OF BLESSING IN THE OLD TESTAMENT

The Hebrew word for blessing is *berakah*. *Berakah* was of
great importance in the life of Israel. A blessing conveyed
the personal energy of the one who gave it. It "contained
its own energy of fulfillment; he who was blessed received
this energy into his own soul" (Herbert, 1962:26). *Berakah*
was a solemn, deliberate act through which specific and concrete blessings were given.

Blessing is a power-laden concept. The term may refer to
the power inherent in spoken words, to the words themselves,
or to the effects they have on the hearers. Words of blessing were usually "spoken on cultic or other occasions and
often were accompanied by gestures or symbolic actions,
through which the wholeness of the religious community was
understood to be safeguarded or strengthened, and evil forces
controlled or destroyed" (Harrelson, 1962:446).

Because of the power connected with blessing in the Old
Testament, because of the many parallels between Old Testament
power concepts and similar concepts in Babylonian and Phoeni-
cian religions, some people believe that blessing is related

to a primitive form of magic. They see blessing as something definitive and objective, quantitative rather than qualitative. They focus on Israel's struggle with a strong animistic emphasis on blessing, much like many Muslims in West Africa today who struggle with the tension between animistic and classical emphases and interpretations of blessing.

Numbers 22:6 indicates that in pre-Israelite days blessing was thought of as a magical formula or power. Balak believed that Balaam possessed this power. But as the story unfolds, we see that blessing was a prerogative of God. Balaam does not possess it as a magical power to be used irrespective of God. Thus, when God blessed the people of Israel, Balaam would not curse them as he had been sent to do. All he does is confirm God's blessing on them, much to the dismay of Balak.

Von Rad sums it up well. He declares that one does not understand the substance of the Old Testament concept of blessing "if one proceeds primarily from the notion of a magically effective manistic 'strength of mind' which is poured out like a fluid" (Von Rad, 1972:159).

Blessing is not magic, but it is power, power that is given to man by God. Pedersen (1926) calls attention to the fact that blessing is an element of vitality. It is seen in the Old Testament as a life-power which saturates the soul. Not only is the degree of blessing different from person to person, but the kind of blessing differs as well between people. But all types of blessing have one thing in common: they are concerned with the positive use of God's power.

The concept of blessing is filled with power that has definite purposes. It is given to man to be used by him for the purpose of glorifying God and for the continuation of his existence. Therefore, it is not a narrow concept, but includes several ingredients. The major aspects of blessing are fertility and prosperity, *shalom*, holiness, and praise and thanksgiving.

Fertility and Prosperity

One basic content of blessing in the Old Testament is fertility (some prefer the word fertilization); that is, the power to multiply. Each living part of God's creation is given the power to reproduce. When God created man and woman, his first command to them was: "Be fruitful and multiply." The book of Genesis constantly repeats this potent theme.

Noah receives the blessing when he leaves the ark (Gen. 9).
Abraham receives the promise of blessing on his departure
from Ur: "And I will make of you a great nation, and I will
bless you, and make your name great so that you will be a
blessing" (Gen. 12:2). Isaac receives this promise too:
"Fear not, for I am with you and will bless you and multiply
your descendants for my servant Abraham's sake" (Gen. 26:24).

The powerful theme marches on through history to Jacob
who hears the voice of God say, "I am God Almighty; be
fruitful and multiply; a nation and a company of nations
shall come from you, and kings shall spring from you. The
land which I gave to Abraham and Isaac I will give to you,
and I will give the land to your descendants after you"
(Gen. 35:11-12).

Not only is the power to reproduce a blessing, but the
children themselves are blessings. As Psalm 127:3-5 says,

> Lo, sons are a heritage from the Lord, the fruit of the
> womb a reward. Like arrows in the hand of a warrior are
> the sons of one's youth. Happy (blessed) is the man who
> has his quiver full of them. He shall not be put to
> shame when he speaks with his enemies in the gate.

To be blessed is to have a large progeny. The deepest hope
of the people of Israel, their supreme desire, was to be
numerous, to spread over the face of the earth. David confirms this strong desire for blessing, "Now therefore may it
please thee to bless the house of thy servant, that it may
continue forever before thee; for thou, O Lord God, hast
spoken, and with thy blessing shall the house of thy servant
be blessed forever" (2 Sam. 2:29).

The deep concern for passing on, for the continuation of
the family blessing, is most dramatically portrayed in the
conflict between Esau and Jacob. Isaac wanted to pass on
the potential for descendants so that his name and life
would be preserved and continued. His blessing was not mere
words. Once uttered it was humanly impossible to revoke the
words and the power they carried. That explains why Esau
was extremely angry. It was Jacob who now carried within
him the potential for innumerable descendants, for prosperity,
for lordship, for charisma-filled leadership. It could not
be retransferred to Esau. When Isaac spoke the words of
blessing, something real happened; some indefinable power and
gift had been given to Jacob.

But the children of Abraham were not just passive recipi-
ents of blessing. They often had to participate in acts of
blessing and cooperate with God in the act of bestowing
blessing. "The blessing has a certain independence of man,
in that it is not controllable by him, yet at the same time
its transmission requires the cooperation of man in its pronouncement" (Mowvley, 1965:76).

An explicit example of this fact is the role that the blind
old man Isaac plays in the passing on of the paternal blessing
of Abraham to his son. "Without question the effectiveness
of this blessing, according to the conception of our narra-
tive, does not rest with God only but requires active giving
on man's part and a special will to give it to a younger man.
Objective and subjective elements are here inseparably bound
together" (Von Rad, 1972:276).

Shalom

Another important part of the content of blessing is peace,
wholeness, and health. These words are definitions of the
widely used term *shalom*. *Shalom* is a word that is found in
the context of everyday life and is the object of the most
profound religious expectations.

Shalom is today, as it was in Old Testament times, a common greeting. It seems to involve blessing or concern for
another's personal welfare. Thus we see in the Old Testament
how Joseph asks his brothers, when they came to Egypt, "Is
your father well?" (Gen. 43:27).

In addition to the concern for personal well-being, *shalom*
is often used to speak about the well-being or welfare of
a city, a nation, even the whole world. God promised his
people, "I will give *shalom* in the land, and you shall lie
down, and none shall make you afraid" (Lev. 26:6). Years
later when the people were taken into captivity and exile
because of their disobedience, Jeremiah told them, "Seek the
welfare (*shalom*) of the city where I have sent you into exile,
and pray to the Lord on its behalf, for in its *shalom* you will
find your *shalom*" (Jer. 29:7).

Shalom means wholeness, completeness. It means a world
functioning as God intended it to function. It is seen in
the Old Testament as a gift of God. Men cannot earn *shalom*,
although they certainly can ruin this gift of blessing. Israel herself is an example of this fact. God delivered the
people of Israel from bondage and slavery in Egypt. He

brought them to the promised land and gave them peace and
blessing. As long as they served him faithfully, they en-
joyed *shalom*. But when they forgot what God had done for
them, when they turned to their own goals, Israel lost *shalom*.
Instead of living in peace and contentment, they lived in a
land wracked by war and internal strife. They were finally
taken into captivity.

These events indicate that *shalom* is a vital part of blessing. When *shalom* is active in a person's or community's or
nation's life, there is health, wholeness, and peace.

Holiness

An additional significant aspect or corollary of blessing
is the concept of holiness. Holiness is related to *shalom* in
that, in one way, it grew out of the context of war and peace.
Because the soldiers of Israel had God, the Holy One, as their
commander-in-chief, because he gave them the desire and power
to win his battles, the Israelites called the warrior's state
qodesh, holiness.

Holiness was seen as a common force impregnating all the
warriors of Israel. Not only themselves, but everything they
possessed was pervaded by this same force. The soldiers were
called the "sanctified of Yahweh" (Isa. 13:3) because they
were blessed with the power of holiness. Even their weapons
and military encampments were considered sacred as long as
they themselves were in a war-like state (1 Sam. 21:6; Jer.
27:7) (Pedersen, 1940:12).

But the weapons themselves were not the deciding issue in
war. Of greater importance was the fact that the soldiers
possessed *berakah*, that the impact of holiness was active in
their lives. And even more crucial was the necessity for the
leader to be charisma-filled. As the natural leader (chief,
judge, king), he was filled with the Spirit of Yahweh. As
the appointed and anointed leader of God's people, he had the
responsibility of keeping the holiness of his army intact.

In the narratives of Saul and David we see an explicit
picture of the far-reaching impact of holiness. As Saul
begins to turn more and more in on himself, and away from
obedience to God, he loses control of his people. The aura
of holiness which had surrounded his life and personality
diminishes, and in the end, he perishes in his struggle to
uphold the blessing. Out of Saul's ruin David rises. David
is filled with blessing and holiness and is "ready to give an

entirely new foundation to Israelite life by instituting a
monarchy which had not previously been seen in Israel" (Pedersen, 1940:46).

The dynamic impact of holiness is seen in people other
than those involved in military leadership. Priests were
declared holy in a special ceremony in which they are set
apart for special service to God (Exod. 29). Their holiness
was dependent on their relationship to God, the Holy One.
The mainspring and controlling principle of holiness is the
realization of God's true character. "You shall be holy; for
I the Lord your God am holy" (Lev. 19:1). To retain this
gift of God and to be respected as special, holy people by
others, the priests had to live lives of moral conduct and
righteousness.

Prophets were also called holy men of God (2 Kgs. 4;9).
They received the gift of holiness through being appointed
by God for specific sacred tasks. Jeremiah was greatly respected as a holy man. The people knew that God had chosen
him to bring them a sacred message they needed to hear.
"Before I formed you in the womb I knew you, and before you
were born I consecrated you; I appointed you a prophet to
the nations' (Jer. 1:4).

Certain men were set apart for sacred service among the
people of Israel. Called the Nazirites, they became accepted
as holy men because they were separated from and set apart
for special ministries. Samson and Samuel are two such
Nazirites. Because they were set apart for a time, they
were viewed as holy (Num. 6:5).

Thus, we see that holiness was an important aspect of
blessing in that it communicated to the people an awesome
sense of the presence and purpose of God. In those who
were viewed as holy men, the people felt the nearness and
holiness of God. They believed that through intimate contact
and relationship with these holy men, they, in turn, would
receive the blessing of God.

Praise and Thanksgiving

In most occurrences of the word, man is the receiver of
blessing. He is given the power to be fruitful and multiply.
Prosperity, *shalom*, and holiness are gifts that are given
to him by God. But there is an aspect, a meaning, of blessing
in which man blesses God. To bless God is to respond to his
goodness, love, and mercy with words and actions of praise

and thanksgiving. In blessing God, man gives or offers to
God that which is most beneficial to himself. The Psalms,
in particular, abound with expressions of blessing as praise
and thanksgiving to God.

THE CONTENT OF BLESSING IN THE NEW TESTAMENT

While a theology of blessing is not overtly developed in
the New Testament, the consistent rephrasing of the intent
and impact of blessing reveals its importance. We see in the
New Testament that the concept of blessing is characterized
by both a retention of significant Old Testament aspects and
by a transformation of meaning resulting in Christological
emphases. The beauty of the New Testament is revealed in the
balanced blending of the two.

Continuity of Content from the Old Testament

We have already seen in the blessings of Jesus that as a
true Jew he was greatly influenced by his culture. The framework of his blessing the children, the food, and his disciples
upon his departure was Jewish. It was natural that Jesus, a
Jew, perform such acts.

Similar aspects of the Old Testament understanding of
blessing are revealed in the lives of other New Testament
characters. Some key aspects obtained from the Old Testament are those of fertility, growth and maturity, and peace.

Fertility. We discovered in our study of the Old Testament
that fertility was a major aspect of blessing. God's first
command to mankind was to be fruitful and multiply. He promised Abraham many descendants. The fulfillment of that
promise required a special intervention of God to make Sarah's
barren womb fertile. In the New Testament we see a similar
intervention of God in the lives of two women.

Elizabeth, the wife of Zechariah, was unable to bear children until God blessed her with fertility in old age. Her
pregnancy was viewed by her husband and by the people as a
special blessing of God. "Zecharias receives the higher
blessing for which he prayed" (Plummer, 1922:12). But his
lack of faith resulted in temporary punishment by dumbness.
After the birth of his son, John the Baptist, Zechariah's
tongue is loosened and he blesses God for his marvelous intervention.

The second woman who received a blessing of fertility from
God was Mary, the mother of Jesus. Her special blessing was

the unique role and function she was to have in the plan and
purposes of God. The conversation and greeting of praise
that took place when Mary visited Elizabeth (Luke 1:39f) indicates the deep sensitivity that Elizabeth had for God's
blessing. Knowing that she herself had been blessed like
Abraham's wife, Elizabeth realizes that God had worked an
even greater blessing of fertility in Mary.

Growth and maturity. In addition to fertility, one finds
several references to the ongoing blessing of God seen in
growth and maturity. It is said of John the Baptist that
"the child grew and became strong in spirit, and he was in
the wilderness till the day of his manifestation to Israel"
(Luke 1:80). There are similar references to Jesus: "The
child grew and became strong, filled with wisdom; and the
favor of God was upon him" (Luke 2:40). The blessing (favor)
of God is presented by Luke as an underlying, inconspicuous
but crucially important, activity of God. The fact that Luke
records this blessing of growth and maturity two times in
Jesus' life (the second time is Luke 2:52) indicates the importance of blessing in the New Testament.

A further, though not explicitly stated, evidence of growth
and maturity as an aspect of blessing is seen in Jesus blessing the children. The fact that the Synoptic writers did not
deem it necessary to explain the "why" of the act indicates
that the blessing was a normal event. It also indicates that
the activity of Jesus was not only for adults. Blessing is
not something that is static; it is not primarily event-
oriented. Blessing as growth and maturity is a process of
becoming. The account of Jesus blessing the children, according to Westerman (1978),

> expresses the truth that in order to hear the proclamation
> of the kingdom of God and to respond to it, a person must
> first be born, be a small child, and grow. The work of
> Jesus includes this creaturely side of our humanity, and
> therefore he is not only the one who saves and who pro-
> claims salvation in the coming of the kingdom, but is also
> the one who blesses (p. 85).

Peace. Of the promises and blessings that Jesus shared
with his disciples immediately before and after his death and
resurrection, three stand out as being significant: presence,
power and peace. While all three find their roots and ante-
cedents in the Old Testament, peace, more than the others,
stands firm in the traditions and theology of the Old Testament. In both content and form, peace remains basically the

same in the New Testament as it was in the Old Testament.
Because of this fact, "it is not possible to trace any development of the idea of *eirene* within the NT" (Beck and Brown,
1976:780). If there is any change at all, it is a deepening
of the Old Testament idea of peace, an extension and broaden-
ing of *shalom* (Gross, 1970:650).

In the New Testament, the major emphasis of peace is the
idea of wholeness. As wholeness, peace brings a newness to
human relationships (2 Cor. 5:17; Gal. 6:15). Peace is an
essential concomitant of the Kingdom of God. The Kingdom of
God blesses people with peace in the sense that it creates
unity and harmony between men and God as well. It is ground-
ed in the redemption of Christ. He is the giver and mediator
of peace (John 14:27). The well-being of the early Church
is described as peace (Acts 9:31).

In the New Testament we also find a close tie between
blessing and peace in greetings and benedictions. "Grace be
to you and peace..." was a common greeting. The writers of
the epistles opened many of their letters with words of peace.
While "grace" is the word used most often in farewell greetings, one finds some use of peace as well: (Rom. 15:33; 1 Pet.
5:14; 3 John 15).

New Aspects of Content in the New Testament

When some scholars have studied the concept of blessing in
the New Testament, they have concluded that blessing has the
same meaning as it does in the Old Testament. True, we have
seen many similarities already. But we cannot agree with
scholars like Schenk who conclude that these passages "show
that the concept is found in the New Testament merely as Old
Testament, Jewish material and has no longer any distinctive
meaning (significance) of its own" (Schenk, 1967:132). Our
study indicates that the New Testament significantly changes,
modifies, and transforms several aspects of the concept of
blessing. This change and expansion is seen most vividly
in studying the concept of blessing in the New Testament.

Inheritance of God's kingdom. While the idea of inheriting
the blessing of God is based on the historical fact of God's
blessing of Abraham, the New Testament applies the idea of
inheritance to the Kingdom of God. We see this emphasis immediately in the first occasion when Jesus blessed--the blessing of the children. All three Synoptic accounts highlight the
blessing of the children as the opening of an entrance to the
Kingdom of God. In all three pericopes Jesus is telling the

adults that in order to hear the proclamation of the Kingdom
and to respond in faith by entering, one must become as a
little child. It is an astonishing statement: the child is
the model, not the adult.

In blessing the children, Jesus is highlighting the tremendous fact that we must come to God in humility and un-
questioning faith.

To receive the kingdom and to enter into it are not diverse
actions when we remember what the kingdom is, namely, the
working of his power and his grace wherever he is present.
This we receive, i.e., as a gift. God bestows his grace
upon us; and thus we enter the circle, the domain, where
God works with his grace. By receiving the kingdom we
enter into it, and by entering into it we receive it.
(Lenksi, 1946a:428)

In inheriting the Kingdom of God, children and adults
alike receive the rule and lordship of God. "The Kingdom of
God is His kingship, His rule, His authority" (Ladd, 1959:21).
Having God as ruler and Lord in our lives is not a once-in-
a-lifetime event. It is an ongoing phenomenon, a continuing
blessing. No matter at what stage in our lives, whether as
children or as older adults, we enter the Kingdom of God--
that realm of God's blessing-- we do so through grace and
faith. In being under God's rule, his blessing to us is
both present and future.

The kingdom of God is God's sovereign reign; but God's
reign expresses itself in different stages throughout
redemptive history. Therefore, men may enter into the
realm of God's reign in its several stages of manifestation and experience the blessings of His reign in differ-
ing degrees. God's kingdom is the realm of the Age to
come, popularly called heaven; then we shall realize the
blessings of His Kingdom (reign) in the perfection of their
fulness. But the kingdom is here and now. There is a
realm of spiritual blessing into which we may enter today
and enjoy in part but in reality the blessings of God's
kingdom (Ladd, 1959:22-23).

It is in the close relationship between the Kingdom of God
and blessing that we see the eschatological dimension of the
New Testament's thrust. This dimension is vividly portrayed
by Jesus in his parable of the last judgment (Matt. 25:31-46).
The entire passage is a picture of the contrast of blessing
and cursing. It is the blessed ones who inherit the Kingdom

because they are identified with Jesus Christ who is *the*
heir (Rom. 8:17).

The Kingdom is not given to the blessed ones because of
their works of mercy. No, they inherit the Kingdom. An
inheritance is not a reward for merit or good works. This
does not deny the importance of good works of love and mercy.
But Matthew makes it clear that, for him, the highest blessing is entry into the Kingdom of God and eternal life (Matt.
25:46). "In this last judgment scene the meaning of the
blessing cannot be mistaken: no material gifts are included,
no political dreams are realized. The blessing consists of
the inheritance into God's kingdom" (Van den Doel, 1968:156).

Grace, forgiveness, and reconciliation. In the act of deliverance in Christ, one receives the grace of God, the forgiveness of sins, and is reconciled with God. In this initial
act of faith, which we call the new birth or salvation, God
makes us his children. He creates a covenant between himself
and us. But that is not the end of the story, only the beginning. Grace, forgiveness, and reconciliation become part
of God's ongoing blessing in the continuation of discipleship. We need God's grace anew each day. We are to confess
our sins and receive God's forgiveness every morning. Life
is an ongoing process of reconciliation and renewal because
of man's ups and downs. All this ongoing action takes place
within the covenantal relationship that God established with
man. It is within this relationship that the dynamic role of
blessing is so strategic in the life of the Christian and
that of the Church.

Not only does the believer receive the blessing of grace,
forgiveness, and reconciliation in his daily walk with God;
he is commanded by the Lord to share them with others, even
his enemies. Jesus exhorted his followers, "Love your enemies, do good to those who hate you, bless those who curse
you, pray for those who abuse you" (Luke 6:27-28). In this
passage and its parallels, Jesus takes the essentials of salvation and expands them to become the continuous acts of
blessing required of a follower. It is in such passages that
we see the dynamic and necessary tension between salvation
and blessing.

Gift of the Holy Spirit. We have previously seen that the
concept of blessing is both intimately related to the act of
salvation in Christ and yet is distinct from it. This fact
is especially evident when we explore a third aspect of
blessing and its content, the gift of the Holy Spirit. The

fact that the Holy Spirit is part of the content of blessing is seen in the farewell words of Jesus and in the theology of Paul.

A study of the New Testament shows that the relationship between Jesus and the Holy Spirit was not static, but rather a dynamic one. This relationship can be seen in three developing stages.

First, Jesus as man is the creation of the Spirit. Jesus was conceived by the power of the Holy Spirit, as Matt. 1:20 states and the Apostles' Creed confesses. The incarnation was an overt act of the Holy Spirit.

Secondly, Jesus is the anointed man of the Spirit. At his baptism the Holy Spirit descended upon him and began to lead him in his life. From that moment on, the Holy Spirit was the power of God in Jesus' life. In addition to his birth and baptism, every stage of his life and ministry was associated with the Spirit: temptations (Mark 1:12); preaching (Luke 4:18-21); miracles and exorcism of demons (Matt. 12:28); and death (Heb. 9:14).

Thirdly, in his death and resurrection, a transformation takes place and Jesus becomes the Lord and giver of the Holy Spirit. At the moment of his ascension he gives his disciples irrefutable evidence that he has become the blesser, the giver of the Holy Spirit. In blessing his disciples he says, "But you shall receive power when the Holy Spirit has come upon you; and you shall be my witnesses...." (Acts 1:8). The dsiciples understood that Jesus had become the giver of the Holy Spirit because they remembered the penetrating words Jesus had spoken in the upper room, "It is to your advantage that I go away, for if I do not go away, the Counselor will not come to you; but if I go, I will send him to you" (John 16:7). After Jesus' ascension, the disciples returned to Jerusalem being assured that the empowering blessing of the Holy Spirit was soon to come upon them.

The Apostle Paul refers to the Holy Spirit as part of the content of blessing in two related passages. These passages are Rom. 15:29 and Gal. 3:1-14.

In the conclusion of his letter to the Romans, Paul is describing his intense desire to visit them, for he will come "in the fulness of the blessing of Christ" (Rom. 15:29). What this passage actually means is debated by scholars. Some focus on the results of the blessing in the life of the

Church. For example, "By this he means great success and
growth" (Calvin, 1961:316). However, this emphasis does not
completely fulfill Paul's intent which he shared in the introduction to his letter. His hope was to "impart some spiritual gift" (Rom. 1:11). Clarke (n.d.) is much closer to a
complete understanding when he states that Paul hoped to come
to the Romans "endowed with the gifts and graces of the Lord
Jesus himself" (p. 160). Murray (1968) sums it up well:

> We are liable to think of the rich blessing that would
> accompany his ministry. This is without doubt in view.
> But we may not restrict the thought thus. The terms
> indicate that he will come thither in the possession of
> the fullness of Christ's blessing. This evinces the
> confidence of Christ's abiding presence in the plenitude
> of his grace and power (p. 220).

The Apostle Paul adds credence to the fact that the Holy
Spirit is part of the content of blessing when he sets out
to interpret the blessing of Abraham in Gal. 3:1-14. In
verses 1-5 he states explicitly that we receive the Spirit
by faith. He continues in verse nine by asserting that "those
who are men of faith are blessed with Abraham who had faith."
In the conclusion of this section, Paul confirms for us the
conviction that the Holy Spirit is the content of blessing.
"In Christ Jesus the blessing of Abraham might come upon the
Gentiles, that we might receive the promise of the Spirit
through faith" (3:14).

6

How Blessing
is Communicated

Blessing is not an automatic power that forces itself on
people. The power of blessing is bestowed by God on his
people. But he does not bestow it only on special occasions.
Because he established his covenant with his chosen people,
God is ready to give his blessing on a regular basis. It is
true that continual blessing demands obedience, but this
obedience on the part of people is always within the context
of covenant.

But how did God communicate his blessing to people? What
forms did spiritual leaders of Israel and the early Church
use to bring God's blessings? A study of the forms of blessing reveals two basic modes of communication: the spoken word
and sacred acts.

COMMUNICATING BLESSING THROUGH THE SPOKEN WORD

A common mode of communicating God's blessing was through
the spoken word. We see in the Old Testament that the Hebrews
believed that the spoken word communicated power and had great
impact. When a word of blessing was uttered, it usually could
not be retracted. In expressing himself, the speaker goes
outside himself and imposes himself on others. This emphasis
in the Old Testament is seen in the word *dabar*. Leenhardt
(1955) provides an excellent discussion of the relationship
between outward expression and inward intent. Focusing on the
intent of the communication, he says, "The first meaning of
the term *dabar* is 'to be behind and to push forward....' For
when man speaks there is something which is 'behind,' still

hidden, and which pushes forward. The words are pushed outside by what is 'behind,' the secret thought" (p. 263). In
other words, when man speaks, he also acts. "For the Hebrew
speech is speech plus (or rather which is) act" (Beaty, 1963:
58). In language there is an act of power, a manifestation
of authority (Leenhardt, 1955:266).

Pedersen (1926) speaks of the spoken word as an expression
of the soul. "The power of the word consists entirely in its
mental essence. The word is the form of vesture of the contents of the soul, its bodily expression.... He who utters a
word to another lays that which he has created in his own
soul into that of the other, and here then must it act with
the whole of the reality it contains" (p. 167).

Thus, when God or one of his chosen servants (not just
anyone) pronounced a blessing, it was not mere words. It
conveyed the essence of his being. In the spoken word, what
he possessed was transported and given to the hearer who was
open to receive it. The spoken word was effective because of
the authority of the speaker.

We see the communication of blessing through the spoken
word in three main forms: benedictions, greetings, and beatitudes. Through these spoken media the power and blessing of
God were bestowed upon his people.

Benedictions

A common way to give someone a blessing was through the
utterance of a verbal benediction. Depending on the era involved, the benediction was pronounced primarily by a father
to his children, by someone in authority, by a priest to the
people, or by an epistle writer. The benediction always
included God's name.

In the patriarchal period of Israel's history, the great
concern was for the continuation of the people of God. The
covenant that God made with Abraham had been impressed upon
the hearts and lives of his family. They were deeply conscious of the necessity, at all costs, of making sure that
Abraham's lineage be promulgated. They wanted to pass on the
blessing of Abraham. Even though in later traditions the
blessing of Abraham was understood as having descended from
him to "all the communities of the earth (Acts, 3:25; Gal.
3:8)" (Vawter, 1977:177), the family of Abraham had as its
immediate concern the preserving and transferring of God's
blessing on Abraham, and through the process of inheritance,
on them as well.

The most explicit example of this deep concern for the transferring of the blessing of Abraham is found in the account of Isaac as he is nearing death. As the head of the family, he is, in the minds of the Israelites, the center of its soul. "It is the soul which is translated to the heir, i.e., he is invested with all the authority of the giver of the blessing, in addition to which wishes are uttered that the blessed should grow greater than the giver of the blessing" (Murtonen, 1959:161). Even though Isaac was misled and deceived when Jacob cunningly took Esau's place and received the blessing, in the end it didn't really matter because behind the blessing was God, the source and giver of blessing. He was the final authority.

The benediction carried with it not only the assurance of blessing, but, within the worship setting, became a means or medium of blessing. In the New Testament we find both homiletic benedictions and the apostolic benediction. The impact of the homiletic benediction was that the word as spoken, preached, and taught was from God himself. The blessing could not end with this benediction if it were simply a human discourse on some interesting subject. The homiletic benediction was a witness to and a channel of the impartation of God's blessing on the hearers and readers of the Word of God.

The Apostolic Benediction is found in 2 Cor. 13:14: "The grace of the Lord Jesus Christ and the love of God and the fellowship of the Holy Spirit be with you all." There is a close relationship between this benediction and the Aaronic Benediction (Num. 6:24-26). The older Aaronic Benediction declares the fact of God's blessing, grace, and peace, while the Apostolic Benediction presents the cause of this fact and the means through which the blessing, grace, and peace given through Christ are realized by God's children (Dolbeer, 1907: 78-79).

Greetings

In the biblical accounts every greeting was a blessing. When people met each other and exchanged greetings, there was an actual encounter of presence and power. A greeting was an I-Thou encounter in which the I makes himself and all that he possesses available to the Thou. The word spoken in a greeting, in an I-Thou encounter, always had a good intention. It was meant to convey the I's concern for the welfare of the Thou.

We see this in Abraham's encounter with the three strangers
who came to announce the promise of a son (Gen. 18). Even
though the three are strangers to Abraham, his greeting shows
that he makes available to them all that he has and is so
that they feel welcome.

In the New Testament, greetings are either spoken or
written. The written greetings occur either at the beginning
or end of the epistles. The most common initial greeting is
"grace and peace." The significance of this epistolary
greeting is not only the wish that God would grant them his
abundant favor and peace, but that the greeting is expanded
to include the source of blessing: "from God our Father and
the Lord Jesus Christ." Paul and the other writers want to
characterize the exalted value of grace and peace and want
the readers to be sure to acknowledge the source of all
blessings, including the blessing of the epistle itself.

Most of the epistles conclude with a wish and prayer for
the blessing of grace. Through these written forms, the
people received the intent and scope of God's favor and were
reassured that God and his blessing were with them.

Beatitudes

A final form of the spoken word in the Bible is the beatitude. A beatitude is a declaration and proclamation of
blessing and exalted joy. In the Old Testament it is characterized by its fixed form and the use of derivatives of
'ashre, rather than the more common *baruk*. *'Ashre* in the
noun form, which is the most common usage, means "O the
happiness/blessedness of...." The beatitudes occur mostly
in the poetic literature of the Old Testament, especially
Psalms and Proverbs.

In the beatitude, *'ashre* is an introduction to the blessing that the speaker wishes for the hearer. The book of
Psalms begins with a beatitude.

> Blessed is the man who walks not in the counsel of the
> wicked, nor stands in the way of sinners, nor sits in the
> seat of the scoffers; but his delight is in the law of
> the Lord, and on his law he meditates day and night.
> (Psalm 1:1-2)

In these two verses the psalmist is praising him who is
righteous and trusts in God. Other psalmic beatitudes
praise those who are considerate of the needs of others(41:1);

those who are just (106:3); those who revenge Israel against
her enemies (137:8-9).

A beatitude is also pronounced on the man who is fruitful
(127:5), on the one whose sins are forgiven (32:1-2), on one
whom God chastens (94:12), and on one whom God draws near to
himself (72:17). Thus we see that the authors of the Psalms
were deeply conscious and aware of the blessings of God and
amassed a huge collection of beatitudes to express these
blessings.

In the New Testament the fixed word used in all beatitudes
is *makarizo* or one of its various forms. Because of this
fact, some scholars prefer to call the beatitudes "makarisms."
They use this term to show that there are other beatitudes
in the New Testament besides the famous beatitudes of Jesus
in the Sermon on the Mount.

The beatitudes that Jesus spoke. While there were other
times when Jesus communicated blessing in the form of beatitudes (Matt. 11:6; 16:17; Luke 7:23; 11:28; John 20:29), the
most famous of Jesus' beatitudes or makarisms are those in
the Sermon on the Mount. Recorded in Matt. 5:3-12 and Luke
6:20-23, the beatitudes serve as an introduction to a great
moment of teaching by Jesus about the Kingdom of God and what
it means to be in a right relationship of faith and obedience
to God.

A comparison of the two Gospel accounts indicates that
the number of beatitudes in each is different (Matthew has
nine, Luke has four). However, both indicate that Jesus was
using this form of communication to present in realistic,
understandable terms what the road to life with God was like.
It was a life of peace, righteousness, and blessedness designed to be lived within a world that was radically different
from that kind of life.

In the beatitudes, Jesus was trying to tell his disciples
that in receiving salvation and blessing from God, they would
enter a radically different kind of life. This new life would
have God's power and blessing as its source and the final
consummation of the world as its goal. In Christ they would
enter this new life of blessing and become fellow participants
with him in the mission of God.

Other New Testament beatitudes. There are other beatitudes
in the New Testament besides those spoken by Jesus. They
occur mostly in the epistles and Revelation, but a few are

located in the Gospels. Most of these beatitudes that have
a teaching function are related to the coming of God's
Kingdom and what it means for life in the present. Other
beatitudes are words of admiration and praise.

COMMUNICATING BLESSING THROUGH SACRED ACTS

In addition to blessing being communicated through the
spoken word, we find in the Bible that blessings were shared
through actions. Because the actions usually imparted blessing, grace, and the power of God, they are called sacred acts.

It is natural that one's theology of symbols and sacraments
will shape, to a certain extent, one's response to and interpretation of these actions. However, it can be shown that
the various acts involved were part of the communication of
blessing. Both the spoken word and sacred acts will also
be vital elements in the Church's ministry of blessing in
Islamic West Africa.

We shall give attention to three basic types of sacred
acts through which the blessing was imparted in the Bible.
They are the laying on of hands, ritual meals, and anointing.
While the sacraments of the Church are also sacred acts
which bestow blessing, we shall discuss them separately in
Chapter 7.

Laying on of Hands

The use of touch in the Bible to communicate blessing is
predominantly the laying on of hands. There are several
examples of blessing being transferred in this way. In
the Old Testament God commanded Moses to lay his hands on
Joshua so that he might be filled with the "spirit of wisdom"
and be commissioned to become the new leader of the people
of Israel (Num. 27:18). Several passages in Leviticus instruct the priest to lay their hands upon the animal to be
sacrificed to bestow God's blessing on it. Jacob blesses
Ephraim by stretching out his right hand and laying it on
him (Gen. 48:14).

It is understandable that the hand became the symbol of
blessing for the people of Israel. It was a symbol of power.
In military terms the hand denoted the strength of the enemy.
God punishes his people by giving them into the hands of
their enemies (Judg. 2:14; 13:1). The hand is seen as a
symbol of power. This is evident in Gen. 32:11 where Jacob
prays to be delivered from the hand of Esau.

A complementary illustration of the hand being the symbol of power and blessing is seen in the phrase "the hand of God." The hand of God created the heavens and the earth. When God's hand rests on people, they are safe from death and destruction(Ps. 80:17; Ezra 7:6,9,28).

The New Testament also gives ample evidence of the use of the hand in sacred acts. Jesus laid his hands on children and the blessing opened the door to the Kingdom of God for them (Mark 10:13-16). Through the laying on of hands by Ananias, God restored sight to the stricken Saul and conferred on him the Holy Spirit (Acts 9:17). Paul reminds Timothy of the spiritual gifts he had received through the laying on of hands (1 Tim. 4:14; 2 Tim. 1:6).

In this study we shall divide the use of the laying on of hands into three categories, all being categories of blessing. These categories are healing, ordination, and the imparting of the Holy Spirit.

Healing. While healing did not always demand the laying on of hands (Luke 8:43-48), this act was normally associated with healing the sick and the afflicted. Jesus touched the ears of the deaf man and healed him (Mark 7:32-35). He restored sight to a blind man by spitting in his eye and laying his hands on him (Mark 8:22-25). He took hold of Peter's mother-in-law's hand and cast out her fever (Mark 1: 30-31). He stretched out his hand and touched a leper and healed him (Mark 1:40-42). One of the rulers pleaded with Jesus to come to his dying daughter and "lay your hands on her, so that she may be made well and live" (Mark 5:23). In spite of the unbelief of people in his home area, Jesus was able to lay his hands on a few and heal them (Mark 6:5).

The use of hands in healing continued in the early Church. In Acts 3:1-7 Peter heals a man lame from birth by taking hold of his right hand. Acts 9:11 refers to miracles done "by the hands of Paul." Paul restored a young man to life by embracing him (Acts 20: 7-10). The gift of healing was a gift of the Spirit (1 Cor. 12:9) and it normally involved the use of the hands.

Ordination. In ordination, the laying on of hands accompanied the spoken word and prayer. Through this sacred act men of God were set aside for specific holy tasks. The act either imparted or confirmed the presence of the Holy Spirit in their lives.

We see the apostles ordaining the seven deacons of the
Church at Jerusalem, men who were "full of the Spirit and
wisdom" (Acts 6:1-6). The act of laying on of hands confirmed
the presence of the Spirit and became, in addition, a symbol
of new status. While in this particular case the bestowal of
some special charisma is not necessarily implied, "the rite
is taken over from the Old Testament, where it symbolizes the
establishment of some vital connections between two persons,
and the transference of some power or responsibility from one
to the other" (Macgregor, 1954:90).

Following the instruction of the Holy Spirit, Paul and
Barnabas were commissioned or ordained for a specific task,
that of bringing the Gospel to the Gentiles (Acts 13:1-3).
The laying on of hands followed fasting and prayer. This
sacred act was a vital part of the ritual of ordination which
gave them, as it had given the seven deacons, a special function or ministry.

Paul is speaking of Timothy's ordination in 1 Tim. 4:14
and 2 Tim. 1:6. Through the laying on of hands, Timothy was
given the function of the ministry. Through this sacred act
Timothy received charisma which was "the ability to preach,
teach, admonish, and to supervise such work in the churches
for which God gave him both the office and the field for the
full exercise of this gift when...he was ordained...by the
laying on of hands" (Lenski, 1946b:754).

Imparting of the Holy Spirit. In the New Testament we also
find references to the laying on of hands as instrumental in
the giving of the Holy Spirit. These occurrences were special
acts outside the normal event of baptism through which the
Holy Spirit was given. However, they are closely related to
baptism.

In Acts 8:14-17 Peter and John found a group of people in
Samaria who claimed that they had not received the Holy Spirit
in baptism. The two apostles "laid their hands on them and
they received the Holy Spirit." Later, at Ephesus Paul met
with a group of believers who had somehow never heard of the
Holy Spirit. They had only been baptised with John's baptism.
Paul thus laid his hands on them and the Holy Spirit came
upon them (Acts 19:1-6).

We thus see that the act of laying on of hands was a sacred
act through which the blessings of God were given. The hands
of the blesser were not sacred. But through these human in-
struments God bestowed his benediction, power, grace and mercy.

There is naturally a rigorous debate about the efficacy of the laying on of hands in communicating grace, power, and blessing. Some evangelicals with strong symbolic theologies and anti-sacramental fervor see the laying on of hands as a form that is only symbolic of what God actually does. An example of this type of interpretation is Parratt (1969) who says, in rejecting the view that the laying on of hands implies a bestowal of the Spirit or power of blessing, "it is unlikely...that this view can be sustained without straining exegetical ingenuity, and it hardly can be judged to do full justice to the complex usage of the rites in the New Testament" (p. 210).

However, it is the firm conviction of the author that, in the light of the Jewish background of the New Testament and the early Church and with the evidence of the New Testament itself, the laying on of hands was a sacred act through which God bestowed varied blessings.

Ritual Meals

Sometimes an act of blessing was accompanied by the eating of a ritual meal. One may question whether the meal strengthened the blessing, but it was a part of the sacred act that the Old Testament patriarch was following in transferring the blessing to his son.

Blessing can also be transferred to people through their participation in and proximity to sacred places of worship, according to the Old Testament. Through the sacrifices offered by the priests, through the sanctification of the holy altar, the people would be blessed by God because he was present among them.

These sacred acts were ways of helping the people remember who they were and whose they were. God had told them, "In every place where I cause my name to be remembered I will come to you and bless you" (Exod. 20:24). Thus the altar, the tabernacle, the temple, became special holy places where the people of God would receive the blessing of God. There they would bring their sacrifices to praise God. In the house of God they would be blessed (Ps. 118:26).

Anointing

A special sacred ritual that conveyed blessing was the act of anointing. In the Old Testament both Saul and David were anointed by Samuel in order to become kings of Israel. The

ceremony of pouring oil on the king's head was regarded as
sacred. The people viewed anointing as the transferring of
the holiness and virtue of God to the king. It was also
viewed as the act through which they received the Spirit of
the Lord (1 Sam. 16:13; Isa. 61:1).

Like the kings, the high priest was also anointed with
oil. Specific instructions were given by God (Exod. 29:1f)
to consecrate the high priest and his servants. The anointing
was both a sign that God had chosen them for their offices
and a channel through which his Spirit would come upon them.
Through this sacred ritual they were set apart to become
holy, special people who would receive blessing in order to
bestow it on God's people.

The prophet also was anointed with oil. Through this
sacred act he was set apart as God's special spokesman. In
1 Kgs. 19:16 Elijah is commanded by God to anoint Elisha as
the prophet in his place. In Isa. 61:1 the prophet witnesses
to the fact that he received the Spirit of the Lord through
the anointing of God. Through this act he was set apart,
given the special task of meeting the needs of the people
with the word of God.

In the New Testament we find references to two types of
anointing. The first is the anointing of Jesus by God the
Father. The specific act of anointing was a part of his
baptism. "At baptism Jesus received the royal and priestly
anointing which made him the Christ" (Müller, 1975:122-23).

His first act as the Christ (Messiah, the anointed one)
was to go to the synagogue at Nazareth and read from Isa. 61:
1-2. He then proclaimed to the people that this prophecy had
been fulfilled in his person (Luke 4:18-19); see also Acts
4:27; 10:38; Heb. 1:9). This anointing of Jesus was a special endowment of the Holy Spirit. Its roots are in the
anointing of priests, kings, and prophets in the Old Testament.

John's earlier description of anointing in 1 John 2:20,27
indicates a close, if not direct, relationship between
anointing and baptism. For John, the *chrisma* (anointing) was
the gift of the Holy Spirit. In the anointing a believer is
"given a share in the messianic anointing of Jesus. He receives the Holy Spirit, who is able to discern the spirits
(1 John 4:1f; 2:18)" (Müller, 1975:123).

In addition to the spiritual impact of the anointing of Jesus, the New Testament contains two references to anointing by oil to heal the sick. This is the second type of anointing. Mark 6:13 states that the disciples used this sacred act to bring healing to the ill. "And they cast out many demons, and anointed with oil many that were sick and healed them." The spectrum of interpretation of this passage and of Jas. 5:14 is vast. On the one hand, some see this act as a metaphor, a symbolic gesture, or perhaps simply an application of a medicinal balm on those who were sick. For example, Gray (1899) says,

> The New Testament contains no references to anointing as a religious rite, unless, indeed, we ought to infer from Mark 6:13, James 5:14, that magical--and so far religious-- properties were attributed to oil used in anointing the sick.... Anointing occurs repeatedly as a metaphorical term to express a religious idea (p. 172).

On the other hand, Roman Catholic theologians base their sacrament of extreme unction squarely on James 5:14. They see Mark 6:13 as a "foreshadowing, figure or type of the future sacrament" (Palmer, 1958:312). The anointing commended by James is viewed as a sacramental sign. It became a part of the baptismal liturgy by the end of the second century, and then developed into one of their seven sacraments.

While the author does not regard anointing as a sacrament, an act which conveys saving grace, the New Testament indicates that it is more than a symbolic act. The sacred act of anointing is one of the signs that indicate the inauguration of the Kingdom of God. It is one way through which the continuing blessing of God is carried out in the Church.

We see, therefore, that blessing was communicated in several ways in the Bible. It had great impact on those who received its power. The most common arena in which blessing was communicated was that of worship, which we shall now investigate.

7

Blessing in Liturgical Perspective

Along with doctrine and ethics, worship is a basic aspect of religion. It was within the liturgical rituals in the life of Israel and the Church that the people comprehended to a greater degree the deep and holistic impact of blessing.

The description of the Church as "the people of God" indicates immediately the corporate nature of Christianity. A believer in Christ is never just an individual. He is part of a larger community. Basic to the life of this community is the worship of God.

The New Testament verifies this basic aspect of corporate worship. We see that the disciples, after having received the empowering blessing of the Holy Spirit, gathered for the worship of God (Acts 2:46-47). While the matrix of worship in the early Church was Jewish, soon new accents developed because of the impact of the Hellenistic culture and the death and resurrection of Jesus.

The various forms used in biblical worship preserved the necessary balance between accents on redemption and accents on blessing. The responses given by the worshipers revealed God not only as Lord and Savior, but also as blesser. This balance between redemption and blessing within the realm of worship is crucial to the Church's life and mission in West Africa.

BLESSING IN THE ARENA OF WORSHIP

Worship and its rituals may be described as the socially
established and regulated holy acts in which the encounter
and communion of the Deity with the congregation was established, developed, and brought to its ultimate goal.   In
other words, it is a relation in which a "religion becomes a
vitalizing factor as a communion of God and congregation, and
of the members of the congregation amongst themselves" (Mowinckel, 1962:15).   In the liturgy we see the visible expression of the relationship between God and his people.

As the development of liturgy took place among the people
of Israel in the Old Testament, we see them as being the re-
cipients of God's initiative.   The Israelites had only been
gone a few weeks from slavery in Egypt when God set up for
them the tabernacle with its accompanying rituals and regula-
tions.   Israel needed God's power, guidance, and presence.
They knew that they could most appropriately receive it
through liturgical rituals, through worship.   What they wanted and received in worship was blessing.   Through cultic rituals, blessing was created, increased, and secured.

Worship was an event to which an individual could come to
encounter anew his God and Lord.   He could experience fellowship with God, and through participation in and following the
rituals, he could experience a cleansing and empowering in
his life.

Yet, an individual did not develop his relationship with
God by himself.   This grew out of his participation in the
community as a whole.   As a member of the community, he dared
to believe and receive God's power, wisdom, and goodness in
his life.

Incorporated into the cultic community of the amphictyony,
the Israelite experiences in the cultic action the real
self-communication of his God through the priestly proclamation of his holy ordinances, and rejoices in the covenant favour and the covenant promises.   In the festivals
carried out at the sanctuary according to the prescribed
forms he expresses his thanksgiving and petition, his vows
and confession of sin, and in union with the congregation
acquires that feeling of being religiously at home which
enables him to place his own little life trustfully in
God's hand.   Collective cohesion proves itself a reinforce-
ment of the individual's power to shape his own life.
(Eichrodt, 1967:239)

Thus, we see that worship became for the Israelites the major source of renewal and strength. It was a major way of receiving and increasing the power of blessing from God. From the time of the Exodus, it became the priest's task to lead in Israel's worship of God. Aaron became the first high priest and his sons were designated as assistants. The tribe of Levi became the specified group of men who were assigned the responsibility of leading the whole nation in the worship of Almighty God.

While "throughout the Bible it is assumed that the initiative in true worship is God's" (Cranfield, 1958:388), the early Church as community believed that one of its major responsibilities and life-preserving necessities was the worship of the holy, living, gracious, unique God as revealed in Jesus Christ. Worship was a celebration of the continuing presence of Jesus Christ (Matt. 28:20), an acknowledgement of and response to the gracious gifts of God, and participation in the renewing work of the Holy Spirit. "Without the operation of the Spirit Christian worship would be a merely human act...human effort and self-exertion before God" (Delling, 1962:23-24).

To worship God in the most effective, meaningful way, there developed basic rituals and acts through which God could bless the worshipers, and they, in turn, could bless him. We shall study the Old Testament and the New Testament separately to more fully grasp the centrality of blessing within the liturgical life of God's people.

BLESSING WITHIN THE RITES OF ISRAEL

Within the arena of worship in the life of the Israelites, we find two specific ways through which God bestowed his blessings. These two ways are the sacrifices and the priestly blessing.

Sacrifice

Because an important means of securing and increasing blessing was done through the sacrifice, we see developing a complex system of sacrifice in Israel. While sacrifice is a part of all cultic religions, including Islam, it must be viewed in the Old Testament within the context of Israel's covenantal relationship with God.

Sacrifices were not viewed simply as symbolic, ritual acts. The effectiveness of the sacrifice depended on the spirit and

attitude of the offerer. "No plea for forgiveness could be
sincere, if there was no renunciation of the sin in the heart;
no cry for cleansing could have any meaning, if there was
still the purpose to renew the act that brought the stain; no
prayer for communion could be genuinely expressed by a sacrifice, if there was no desire to walk in harmony with God's
will" (Rowley, 1950:91).

Yet, sacrifices could not be made for every sin. For instance, the Torah provided no sacrifice for murder or adul-
tery. Only the direct forgiving intervention of God could
atone for these sins and avert the death penalty that was
prescribed for them. This is why the impact of the Prophet
Isaiah is so great. He proclaims that the Suffering Servant
is the one whose death will become the ultimate sacrifice
that will be potent enough to expiate all sins.

Sacrifice cannot be understood merely as man's approach
to God.

It is also God's approach to him, charged with power. It
thus carries a two-way traffic, and God's readiness to
release power for the blessing of man through this avenue
only waited for the opening of the two-way traffic by man's
approach to him in humility and submission. Yet all the
animal sacrifices failed to meet man's need, since the
sins that most needed cleansing were beyond the range of
their power. A sacrifice greater than any the Law provided and more far-ranging in its power, was therefore
envisaged...one to which it looked forward beyond the Old
Testament itself (Rowley, 1950:110).

Through the acts, words, and symbols used in the sacrificial liturgy, the creative power of God was given to the worshipers. To them it meant renewal, revitalization, and an
increase in strength and power. Because God's power, grace,
and blessing were given through these rituals, they took on
a sacramental nature.

The Priestly Blessing

In addition to blessing being received through the rites
of sacrifices, it was shared when the priest spoke the word
of God and pronounced his name. In Israel there was a real
belief that the spoken word exerted power in a quasi-material
way (Eichrodt, 1961:173). This was particularly true when
that word was the name of God. There thus developed the use
of a formula in which God's name was repeated to increase the

power given. We know this formula as the Priestly Blessing.
In these ritual words the priest was said to have laid God's
name on the people. In Semitic cultures, a name was not only
a means of denoting a person. It was tied to the very existence and being of that person. Thus if God's name were
known or heard, it meant that the recipient was relating
himself to God. "When therefore the priests pronounced a
blessing over Israel in the name of Yahweh, it is more than
the expression of a wish that they be blessed. By laying the
name of Yahweh on the people they are in fact setting in
motion an actual beneficient power" (Eichrodt, 1961:207).

The setting of the priestly blessing was usually in the
sanctuary. Sometimes in Hebrew worship it was uttered when
the worshipers entered the house of worship (Ps. 118:26).
But usually it was reserved for the end of the service. We
know it became a prominent part of the liturgy because of the
use of its vocabulary in the Psalter. Various formulations
of blessing-prayers are found in the Psalms (29:11; 67:1;
115:13f; 134:3, for example).

The concept of blessing was not new to the people of God
when Moses gave the responsibility of blessing the people to
Aaron. Up to this point, blessing had been the task of the
father in the family. However, the concept of blessing was
now transformed from the family context to that of liturgical
rituals. It became a vital part of the organized worship
pattern of the people. This solemn declaration (priestly
blessing) became the voice of God in the liturgy. Hearing
these holy words pronounced by the priest meant receiving
the life-creating and life-supporting power of God.

When Aaron was solemnly invested with the priesthood, "he
lifted up his hands toward the people and blessed them" (Lev.
9:22). Then Moses joined him in the sacred tent. When they
came out and blessed the people again, the glory of God appeared to all the people. They knew that this experience was
a direct encounter with God. God's name had been laid on them.

There are three particular and important characteristics
of the priestly blessing. They add insight into the meaning
and function of blessing.

First, we see that the pronoun used is the second person
singular. This indicates the personal, intimate relationship
between the Lord and his people. Its use had a two-fold impact on the worshipper. Not only did he feel that he as an
individual was being blessed by God and in close contact with

him, but that the worshiping community was seen as a "person,"
and became a fellow inheritor of the collective blessings of
God.

Secondly, God's name is repeated in each line. This makes
it clear to all that God is the giver of the blessing. There
is no way possible for the priest to begin thinking that he
is the blesser. This three-fold emphasis was designed to
prevent the people from adoring the human voice of God's
blessing.

Thirdly, the Aaronic Benediction is not a prayer with
three petitions. Rather than a prayer, the benediction is
a proclamation. It is not a wish but a declarative statement.
The word "may" should not be added at the beginning. It is
a blessing. People who hear these words are expecting to
receive God's blessing and beneficient power as they leave
the worship. The benediction is "the Lord's response with
his gracious blessing to the believer and worshiper, and the
act is designed to be a means in the communication of that
blessing" (Dolbeer, 1907:31).

In the context of worship, the priestly blessing soon became a fixed part of the closing portion of worship. This
is significant in that the blessing was seen as a "bridge
from the sacral act of worship in the sanctuary to the life
outside" (Miller, 1975:249). The people came out of the worship experience empowered, rejuvenated, to face the problems
of daily life. In pronouncing the words of blessing on the
people, the priest was telling them that the God whom they
came to worship, the Holy One of Israel, was now going with
them. This final trumpeting message impelled the people to
leave with the confidence and hope that God would care for
them in all the areas of their lives.

In the worship experience in general, and in the priestly
blessing in particular, the people of Israel touched base
with the power, presence, and providence of God. Through the
sacrificial rituals and the proclamation of the blessing,
people encountered God personally and corporately, and they
left empowered for life and service. The priestly blessing
"gives expression in a very few words to the full scope of
God's benevolent designs toward his people, and the means
He has taken to secure the accomplishment of those designs"
(Dolbeer, 1907:38). In the Old Testament the Aaronic Benediction is the ultimate and most complete expression of blessing in liturgical perspective.

BLESSING IN THE RITES OF THE CHURCH

In addition to worship being a service of prayer, praise, and proclamation, the New Testament focuses on the special rites that became a vital part of the worship experience. Two special rites that are the key sacramental rituals of the Church are baptism and the Lord's Supper.

In the New Testament and early Church, we find evidence of these rites being events of blessing. Baptism and the Lord's Supper (Eucharist, Holy Communion) are blessings in that they bring to people God's forgiveness and grace. We call them sacred acts that were commanded and instituted by Christ himself. There are other rites alluded to in the New Testament which later developed in the life of the Church. They can also be called rites of blessing. However, because they were not commanded by Christ and do not convey saving grace, the author does not call them sacraments. But this does not reduce their impact and importance and the blessing of God they can bring. They can rightfully be called "sacramental moments" in that God's presence, promise, and blessing are part of the ritual. We shall briefly examine these special rites in addition to baptism and the Eucharist.

Baptism

In studying baptism in the New Testament, one could conclude that baptism is only an event dealing with symbolic initiation, or at the most, salvation and new life in Christ. Baptism is both of these. Baptism is a symbol of entrance into a new life and into the fellowship of the Church. The words "water" and "washing" in the context of the Church immediately bring to people's minds the act of baptism.

But baptism is more than representative or symbolic. Through this act which Jesus himself experienced, sanctioned, interpreted, and commanded, the blessing of God is bestowed. For sinful human beings, the rite of baptism brings the blessings of forgiveness and the Holy Spirit (Acts 2:38); regeneration (Tit. 3:5); new birth and entrance into the Kingdom of God (John 3:5); and new life (Rom. 6:3-4).

Yet, baptism is not simply individualistic, though it is profoundly personal. "In baptism I come into a relationship not only with God but also with all God's other adopted children"(Brand, 1973:72). The total, overall blessing of baptism is that it brings the new child of God (old or young) into his family. It is the blessing of belonging. It means being a

part of his family and sharing in his mission and ministry.
This is not just an individualistic event. Blessing in baptism introduces one to the journey of the Christian life and
the fellowship of the Christian family.

Baptism is not only the initiation, the entrance into the
Christian life and community. It also provides the continuous dynamic for that life. That is why in the ritual of
baptism, both the application of, or immersion in, water and
the laying on of hands in blessing are vital elements. The
addition of the laying on of hands to the ritual means "that
the one baptized is brought not only under the authority of
God who saves but also into the realm ruled by the God who
blesses" (Westermann, 1978:113).

We thus see that the sacrament of baptism is a special
rite of blessing. It is "no empty symbol or 'bare sign,'
but a genuine sacramental action in which God works, applies
the saving efficacy of the death and resurrection of Christ
in which he died and rose again, and places us in that sphere
of divine life in which sin is conquered" (Martin, 1964:105).
Because of the dynamic role of blessing in baptism, we see
it as a vital ingredient in the growth and outreach of the
individual in the context of community.

The Lord's Supper

The idea of blessing is also basic to the sacrament of
Holy Communion or the Lord's Supper. This is made clear by
the Apostle Paul in 1 Cor. 10:16, "The cup of blessing which we
bless...the bread which we break, (are they not) participation
in the (blood...body) of Christ?" This passage indicates
that from the beginning of the time when the Lord's Supper
was celebrated by the Church, it was viewed and accepted as
an event which imparted God's blessing.

The blessing received in this sacrament is threefold. In
the partaking of the Eucharist, the Christian is blessed with
the forgiveness of sins (Matt. 26:28); he receives the blessing of remembering (1 Cor. 11:25-26); and he discovers the
blessing of fellowship with Christ and the Christian community.

The blessing of forgiveness is an essential factor in
calling the Lord's Supper a sacrament. God's forgiveness is
an act of grace. Thus, as with baptism, the Lord's Supper is
called a means of grace, a means of sacramental blessing.

The blessing of remembering is not original in the New
Testament. The importance of remembering is stressed over
and over in the Old Testament. When Israel remembered God's
act of deliverance and blessing, they had peace and reconciliation (Exod. 13:3; 32:13-14; Ps. 105:5). When they did
not remember God, they lost the blessing and, instead, they
found judgment and war (Judg. 8:34).

Similarly, in the New Testament the remembering of Christ's
love and life brings blessing to the participants in the sacrament. The bread and wine help bring to mind the sacrificial death and liberating resurrection of Christ. If one does
not participate in the sacrament, he tends to forget the
mighty acts of God in Christ, and loses God's blessing.

Receiving the bread and wine in Holy Communion brings one
into an encounter with the risen Christ. His presence is a
vital aspect of the meal. This does not mean that the bread
and wine become magically filled with power. They remain
bread and wine. "It is by the act itself that bread and wine
have the significance which Christ assigned them by his words
and actions" (Elert, 1973:42). Each time believers partake
of the elements of the sacrament, they are eating a special
meal with Christ, and through it, receive his blessing of
renewal.

But participation in the Sacrament of the Altar is not
only a vertical relational event. The believer is also part
of a community. As a celebration of togetherness, the Lord's
Supper brings the blessing of spiritual fellowship and communion. "Because there is one bread, we who are many are one
body, for we all partake of the one bread" (1 Cor. 10:17).
The Lord's Supper is a feast which points beyond to a future
hope of continued blessing and community in the Kingdom of
God.

Other Rites of Blessing

As the Christian Church grew and entered into a more settled life, there developed other special rites of blessing.
While many Christians do not call them sacraments because
they neither bestow saving grace nor are commanded by Christ,
they are special moments when God blesses Christians. While
we do not find actual accounts of these rites in the New Testament, it does speak about their basic premises and spiritual
foundations. The rites we shall briefly include are marriage
and confirmation. We will not include ordination, as that
has already been discussed.

Marriage. God created human beings in his own image, "Male
and female he created them. And God blessed them..." (Gen.
1:27-28). Since this momentous act of creation, union in
marriage has been a ritual and act of blessing. The New Testament, especially in the writings of Paul, focuses on the
union of love as a union of blessing. Marriage was proclaimed
as a blessing, while divorce was a sin and a curse (Matt. 19:
4-9).

But not every marriage is a blessing. God blesses those
who are married because of true love and commitment to him.
With such love as a basis for marriage, one partner is not
more important than the other. While the husband is the
head of the marriage (Eph. 5:23), we can say that the wife
is the heart of the marriage. As life cannot exist without
a head or heart, neither can marriage.

The Christian Church has incorporated the rite of marriage
into its ministry because it sees the importance of guarding
and preserving the centrality of love and blessing. As man
and woman exchange vows and pledge themselves to one another
for a lifelong commitment, the pastor lays his hand on their
hands or on their heads and pronounces words of blessing.
It is in these words that the couple begins their walk together with God as a full partner in their relationship.

Confirmation. The rite of confirmation is practiced by
many Christian Churches as a rite of initiation into adult
membership in the Church. While the Roman Catholic Church
views it as a sacrament, the remaining churches see confirmation as a rite of blessing. The Joint Commission on the
Theology and Practice of Confirmation of the Lutheran Church
defines confirmation as:

A pastoral and educational ministry of the Church that is
designed to help baptized children identify with the life
and mission of the adult Christian community and that is
celebrated in a public rite... In the public rite the
people of God recognize the confirmed as capable of iden-
tifying with the adult Christian community and its mission. They recall with him the event of baptism through
which God, by grace, received him into his Church, and
they testify to the strengthening they receive through the
Word and Holy Communion. The confirmed gives assurance
that he believes the Word and promises of God and affirms
his commitment to the Christian life. The people pray to
God...this prayer may be individualized by the laying on
of hands (Gilbert, 1969:36).

The blessing aspect of confirmation is not only evident in the laying on of hands. The rite itself is a rite of blessing. This is clearly seen in the German word for confirmation, *einsegnung*, which means "imparting a blessing." The aspect of blessing is also seen in the sustaining, growing, ongoing nature of confirmation. Confirmation is blessing because its aim is growth, development, a deepening and maturing of faith and obedience. It is the spiritual expression of the rite of puberty. It is a process, a transition, through which there is new identity with the adult Christian community.

While the New Testament does not speak of confirmation *per se*, it speaks a great deal about growth, mission, maturity, and sanctification, all aspects of the work of blessing. There are several references to the laying on of hands, as we have already seen. This is an "integral act in Christian initiation (which) finds precedent in the life of the Church from its earliest days" (West, 1962:27).

We can best understand blessing in confirmation and other special rites of the Church by seeing blessing as God's continuous activity in the life of his people. As Rom. 7 indicates, the message of the Gospel is not aimed at only one specific event in a person's life. "God's bestowal of blessing is concerned with the whole of human life. It is for this reason that the blessing which accompanies a person throughout life and is bestowed at certain points in the special rites of the Church finds its necessary significance" (Westermann, 1978:117). Marriage and confirmation are two of these special rites of blessing.

Summary

Both the Old and New Testaments contain ample evidence of the centrality and significance of the impact of blessing in the life of the people of God. Blessing was for them God's way of relating to them on a regular basis, assuring them of his presence, power, and grace. Through blessing, people had the potential for growth and maturation. Blessing was a complementary work of God alongside that of deliverance and salvation.

As the Church considers its mission and ministry in the world today, particularly in Islamic West Africa, it dare not think only in soteriological terms. It must view itself also as the communicator of blessing. Through its special rites, sacraments, spoken words, acts of love, and witness, the Christian community can more effectively bring God's holistic blessing to his people at those points in life when they are most needed.

Blessing is intended for a person at a specific point in the trajectory from birth to death. That this blessing is imparted to the Christian community in the name of Christ and is therefore a Christian blessing can be seen in the way in which the specific situation of those assembled is brought into relationship with the work of Jesus Christ and with the church (Westermann, 1978:119).

Our study of blessing has revealed the holistic nature of this potent gift of God. The question we must now ask is: How can we best communicate the blessing of God and the Gospel to Muslims, particularly those living in West Africa?

IV

The Potential of
Blessing in Mission in Africa

From its beginning, this book has had as its intent to focus on the Church's witness and mission to Muslims in West Africa. As it considers its work among Muslims, the Church recognizes that, in spite of sporadic indications of Islamic interest in and conversion to faith in Christ, by and large, West African Muslims remain adamant in their opposition to the good news of the resurrected Christ. There are both theological and cultural reasons for the chasm that exists. Therefore, the Church in West Africa is struggling with the shape of its mission to Muslims in the remaining two decades of this twentieth century.

Our aim has been to further explore one dynamic concept that has great potential for building bridges to Muslims in West Africa. The concept of blessing can become an effective instrument of witness and bridge building because of its centrality both in biblical and Islamic Scriptures and in the everyday life of the believers of the two faiths. Such commonality can reduce or eliminate confrontation or hostility. A Muslim hearing a Christian describe the blessing of God will not reject him. The blessing of God brings Muslims and Christians into a common arena where, hopefully, effective two-way communication, witness, and dialogue can take place.

At the same time, the Church must be careful to distinguish between blessing (*baraka*) that has its source in God and animistic *baraka*. This is often difficult because both types carry the connotation of power. While this may seem

to be an obstacle, it can become an opportunity, because a
"popular" Muslim's sensitivity to power may impel him to
accept the blessing of God in Jesus Christ and discover new
and eternal life.

8

Blessing
as a Bridge to
Islam in West Africa

A number of years ago, while serving the Evangelical Lutheran
Church of Cameroon, I began to sense the potential for focusing greater attention on the concept of blessing in communicating with Muslims. Its tremendous power and influence in
the lives of Muslims was obvious, and it is a key concept in
the Bible and the Christian faith. What was sensed then has
been confirmed in the study that is written here.

This final chapter describes three ways in which blessing
as a holistic, dynamic force can serve as a bridge to Muslims
in West Africa. Naturally, there are other ways in which
blessing will affect the Church's witness. Blessing touches
man at every point of his life. But these three, it seems
to me, may be the most crucial ways for the Church to consider at this point. First, Christians and Muslims alike
look to God as the source of all blessings. This fact, plus
additional factors such as the strong emphasis on the blessing of Abraham, indicate the potential of blessing as a theological bridge to Islam.

Secondly, the influence of blessing through effective
media, personal evangelism, and dialogue reveals the fact
that this concept has become a missiological bridge to Islam.
Finally, and for the author most significantly, the dynamic
impact of ritual indicates that blessing has great potential
as a liturgical bridge to Islam.

BLESSING AS A THEOLOGICAL BRIDGE TO ISLAM

While there are significant theological differences between Islam and Christianity, there are also theological concepts the two faiths have in common. The dynamic power of
blessing is one of these concepts that can become a significant link in building bridges to Islam. The concept of
blessing has promising potential because the two faiths share
the following aspects: God as the source of blessing; the
blessing of Abraham; and the wholism of blessing.

God as the Source of Blessing

As members of the triad of religions that look to God as
the one and only true Deity, Islam and Christianity place a
strong emphasis on the Almighty as the source of true blessing. Of the many features the two faiths have in common,
this one is perhaps one of the most basic ones.

As Muslims and Christians alike reflect on their families,
larger community, lands, nations, and their particular sit-
uations in life, both ascribe praise to God for the richness
of his blessing. Therefore, God as the source of blessing
in both faiths becomes a unifying factor. It is a fact to
which adherents of both religions can radically attest. As
fellow inhabitants of West Africa, they share this common
witness to the animistic and material world around them.

The Blessing of Abraham

The blessing of Abraham is a refined aspect of blessing
that Muslims and Christians treasure and upon which bridges
can be built. Jews, Christians, and Muslims look to the
blessing of Abraham as the beginning of God's gift of covenant and salvation. As the instrument of God's world-wide
blessing, Abraham has become an almost "primal symbol" (Wilken, 1972:275) for Christians and Muslims. Both Old and
New Testaments and the Qur'an contain rich expressions of the
impact of the blessing of Abraham on one's faith in God.

The blessing of Abraham is one significant key that can
unlock the door to a more productive and fraternal relationship between Muslims and Christians. Both are included in the
blessing of Abraham because God's blessing of Abraham was
meant for all the families of the earth. Even though Muslims
and Christians trace the heritage of God's blessing through
different strands, both have Abraham as their common source.
He is the father of both faiths. Those who acknowledge the

blessing of Abraham will be blessed by God. In this way, a
Muslim and Christian in West Africa can come together as
brothers, as children of Abraham, as sharers in the promise
of blessing and its impact on the present and the future.

The blessing of Abraham is more than fertility and land,
as indicated by Nacpil (1968-69):

The blessing that will accrue to mankind by Abraham is
twofold; through him a new style of life--the Abrahamic
style--which in faith is established, and a new and holy
people which will be to God a kingdom of priests will be
formed... a new style of life and the nucleus of a new
humanity shall be the blessing which will come from God
upon mankind through Abraham (p. 177).

Christians need to focus more attention on the blessing of
God in their interaction with Muslims in West Africa. This
is especially true for their initial contacts with Muslims.
Such an approach will result in both Muslims and Christians
reflecting on the power of God's name, because to bless in
God's name is to call upon his power; to bless is to ascribe
to him such power. In the West African context, the blessing of God through Abraham can become a unifying factor that
can help set the stage for friendship, dialogue, mutual trust,
and communication.

The Wholeness of Blessing

Another key aspect of blessing as a theological bridge to
Islam is its holistic impact on the individual and the community. Muslims do not distinguish as clearly as western
Christians between the spiritual and the material, between
the sacred and the profane. They tend to see God's hand of
blessing as touching every aspect of their lives. They have
the innate feeling that the visible world is the outward and
physical sign of inward and spiritual blessing.

This fact is heartening when we realize that the Bible's
emphasis is basically the same. In the Old Testament blessing
is fertility, prosperity, health, and wholeness in addition to
power, peace, and holiness. While the New Testament places
greater emphasis on the spiritual dimensions of blessing, it
does not negate or belittle its impact on the whole of man.

Therefore, blessing can become a significant theological
link between Muslims and Christians when both emphasize the
totality of its role in the individual's and community's life.

If the Christian Church can avoid the polarization and dichotomy of its witness, it can better share with Islamic West
Africans its keen insights into new, eternal ways that God
seeks to bless his people.

BLESSING AS A MISSIOLOGICAL BRIDGE TO ISLAM

The concept of blessing also has great potential for being
a missiological bridge to Muslims. By missiological I mean
communicating the Good News of salvation and abundant life
in Jesus Christ to those who do not know him as Savior and
Lord. Blessing is a central part of this message because
it affects the totality of man's life. Thus, the Church
needs to proclaim the blessing of God in as many ways as
are effectively possible. Three significant ways are through
appropriate media, personal evangelism, and dialogue.

Media

To bring the Gospel to Muslims in West Africa, the Christian Church and mission societies have used television, radio,
films, and cassette tapes as media. These media have their
weaknesses, such as the danger of being man-centered and
exploitative or of a monological, unidirectional nature.
However, their use in West Africa has often been effective as
a beginning strategy. The radio, in particular, has been
instrumental in opening doors to former totally resistant
Muslims. This approach is often followed up or supplemented
by cassette tape ministries and other types of witness.

Those media that have been sensitive to the real needs of
the total person usually have had the greatest impact. As
such, we can say that their ministry is one of blessing in
that it speaks to the multi-faceted needs of living human
beings. With the goal of bestowing *baraka* (material and
spiritual blessings of God), these media can be called incarnational media.

The concept of incarnation fits media of blessing well because through it the word of God becomes incarnated in the
lives of hearers and shares with them its blessing. This is
stressed by Bachman (1976):

The Christian incarnation symbolizes a relationship which
is more conducive to communication. God in Christ has
entered into human affairs, not imposing His will on persons but respecting individual integrity. He demonstrates
the necessity of 'participatory relationships' in communi-

cation but brings into the experience something from beyond. We are invited to follow Him in this precarious
but exciting adventure.... The relationship of incarnation
is based on identification with others.... There are many
individual Christians who are recognized as reconcilers
and who can take the lead in incarnational communication
(p. 14-15).

The concept of media as being incarnation is helpful in
that it recognizes the variety of human needs and personali-
ties. It also insists that the message of blessing be proclaimed within the frame of reference of the receptor people.

The missionary seeking to truly communicate Christ will
find that Jesus' way of choosing to operate within the
cultural frame of reference of his hearers is a much more
enlightened method of communication than the alternative
approach employed by the Judaizers and some western mission
agencies that requires the hearers to accommodate to the
cultural frame of reference of the communicator (Kraft,
1973:283).

Media that bring blessing have as their aim to meet the needs
of the total person as effectively as possible and do it
within the cultural framework of the person.

One example of an effective incarnational medium that has
brought blessings to many listeners in West Africa is Radio
Voice of the Gospel (RVOG). It has broadcast programs in
English, French, Hausa, and Fulani in West Africa. The Hausa
and Fulani programs, in particular, have helped open doors
to further witness among Muslim communities. The author has
personally used the Fulani broadcasts as an initiatory step
to further personal dialogue and witness. Unfortunately, the
Marxist coup in Ethiopia where the transmitters were located
brought an abrupt end to this strategic media ministry in
1977. Other avenues such as cassette tapes are being used
in addition to limited broadcast time over radio station
ELWA in Liberia.

RVOG was effective because its pragmatic messages spoke to
the total person. It avoided the ghetto of traditional Christian broadcasting and became a medium of blessing. Its programs (30% evangelistic and 70% general interest) were cul-
turally relevant in that the communicators and receptors
usually shared common meanings to words and symbols. There
was some difficulty when dialectical linguistic differences
were encountered. Yet, the listeners often identified them-

selves personally with the radio personnel. Pastor Mani-
kasset, the Fulani radio pastor, was called a marabout by
Fulani leaders. As he visited listening audiences, he was
well received and highly acclaimed as a messenger of God.

Among other reasons why RVOG had such an effective ministry
among Fulani Muslims, Jørgensen (1979) lists:

1) The general education level among the Fulani is rather
   low, thus they looked to Sawtu Linjiila (Fulani for
   Voice of the Gospel) for information and education.
2) The majority of Fulani have a naive trust in the ac-
   curacy and truth of what comes to them through the
   media. For them, RVOG was authoritative, and this
   trust carried over into all facets of the broadcasts.
3) At least 90% of the Fulani are Muslim. Christians,
   with some experience among the Fulani where Islam is
   strong, say that they have no way of getting into contact with the Fulani other than by radio.
4) The studio has developed a style and a format which
   through socio-cultural relevance and low-keyed dialogue
   relate to the felt needs of the audience (p. 288).

It is particularly the last reason of Jørgensen that highlights the necessity of media personnel recognizing the importance of seeing themselves as communicators of blessing.
As presenters of the blessing of God and as transmitters of
the Good News of the incarnate one, Christian media serve as
significant factors in the total mission and ministry of the
Church. In the West African context, media have the task of
creating receptivity among Islamic listeners. While the use
of media is never claimed to be the only effective method of
witness, it remains an integral part of a multiple strategy
of witness. Media are important channels of God's incarnational message and communication.

Personal Evangelism

Effective media can contribute to the creation of a more
open attitude to new ideas among West African Muslims. Such
resources can help create new attitudes of friendship and
trust toward Christians and Christianity. But it takes a
personal encounter, a human dialogue, to complete the task
of witness. Therefore, it is crucial that the Church locate
people who have a great love and concern for Muslims and train
them adequately for personal evangelism among their Islamic
friends and neighbors.

The evangelist bringing the Gospel to Muslims must be a
true, honest, faithful messenger of God. He must be recognized as a man of blessing, one who walks closely with God,
one who can be trusted. His life must be filled with empathy and love. He must exhibit an incarnational understanding of Islamic culture and societal relationships. He must
come as a humble yet confident proclaimer of the power of
God. In other words, his stance and message must reveal that
he is blessed by God. All this is significant because his
attitudes toward Muslims will largely determine their attitudes toward him, Christians, and Christianity.

The approach a Christian evangelist takes will be greatly
determined by the type of Muslims to whom he witnesses. If
his Muslim friends and neighbors are stricter, more orthodox
Muslims, settled into a firm routine of obedience to Islamic
laws and traditions, an evangelist's approach may have to
be dialogical. This does not mean engaging in ideological
debate or scholastic controversy necessarily, but rather
sharing faiths. It means working for harmony where a witness
of the Christian faith can be made without seeking religious
syncretism.

A majority of West African Muslims are adherents of what
we have been calling "popular" Islam. A major distinction
between orthodox Islam and "popular" Islam is that in the
latter the felt needs of the people are often met by a com-
bination of animistic-Islamic rituals and methods. Thus,
an evangelist who comes with the Gospel to such Muslims
must exhibit the power of blessing which he has received from
God. The holy power of blessing evident in his life will
communicate to Muslims that he represents Jesus Christ, the
King of Kings and Lord of Lords.

The turning point for adherents of popular Islam is proof
of 'baraka' and power which the evangelist demonstrates.
Understanding of the fundamentals of the gospel is an
event that comes *after* they have confronted Christ and
decided he is indeed Supreme Lord. All they know at the
point of conversion is that *Jesus is powerful* enough to
deal with their problems (Fraser, 1979:173).

Because "popular" Muslims hold beliefs that are often dog-
matically not in harmony with the Qur'an and orthodox Islam,
the evangelist is faced with a tough decision. Should he
seek to lead his "popular" Muslim friend to a new Islamic
faith-allegiance to God; that is, to educate him in his own
faith, as a first step in leading him to faith in Christ?

Or should the evangelist seek a power encounter which, if
successful, will result in a new faith-allegiance directly
to Christ? The choice is not a simple one and the two approaches overlap (Musk, 1979:213-14). If the evangelist
places his primary energies in the second direction he must
be thoroughly prepared to create or provide functional sub-
stitutes for "popular" Islamic practices which cannot be accepted by the Church.

No matter what approach the Christian evangelist uses, he
must come penitently, asking forgiveness for past arrogances,
ridicule, and rejection. He must come with the blessing of
God as revealed in Jesus Christ. Muslims ardently desire
the blessing of God. This gives the evangelist open opportunities through the Muslims' search for this power to lead
them to faith and the abundant life God has promised those
who come to him in faith.

Evangelism to Muslims in West Africa must basically be a
ministry of blessing. Jørgensen (1979) is correct when he
concludes that bringing together the focuses on salvation
and the abundant life that Muslims seek can best be done by
"developing the concept of baraka which Islam and Christianity share with one another" (Appendix 4:20).

An important part of personal evangelism is conveying the
blessing of God through greetings and benedictions. African
Muslims see greetings as significant ways of communicating
and sharing themselves with others. A blessed messenger
of God will widen the spectrum of his witness through careful and proper greetings and benedictions. Within the worship setting or in a family home, greetings and blessing
through the laying on of hands will communicate the love of
God. Its use can build up a Muslim's trust in the evangelist
which will more readily facilitate the reception of the Gospel.

Dialogue

In some instances, the most effective way of bringing the
blessing of God and the Gospel to Muslims is through the communication model of dialogue. Dialogue, a meeting of human
beings in mutual respect, frankness, openness, and sincerity,
may be the tool needed to overcome negative defenses and mistaken ideas Christians and Muslims often have of each other.

Unfortunately, in the past some Christians and Muslims
have viewed dialogue as a tactic to conquer the other person.

At best, Christians and Muslims have tried to attain
knowledge of the other religion, but often with the purpose to defend and attack; at worst, they have looked at
each other with all sorts of misrepresentations, all kinds
of warped images in their minds. A real dialogical openness was the exception on both sides (Mulder, 1977:v).

In dialogue, differences are not surpressed, but rather
explored frankly and critically together by Muslims and
Christians. Participants in dialogue hope for some point of
convergence, not some syncretistic compromise. Vulnerability
is a constant reality in dialogue. However, its presence
should not prevent this two-way communication. In true dialogue, Muslims and Christians are listening for God to speak;
they are searching for his blessing.

A Christian in West Africa dares to dialogue with his Muslim friends because he is inspired by the love of God. He
has the courage to share his faith because he knows that he
and his Muslim friends share many common beliefs and heritages and should carefully listen to one another.

There are threats to honest dialogue. We have already re-
ferred to the potential danger of proselytism and syncretism.
In addition, "the threat may come from presuppositions that
lie behind the twin concerns that 'dialogue is a screen for
proselytizing' and/or that 'dialogue is a form of syncretism"
(Grose, 1976:68).

Used in a dialogical situation, the Great Commission does
not become a teaching, catechetical task. Rather, the task
of the evangelist is to witness, realizing that the convincing power of the Spirit of God is with him. The Church's
task is to witness to the Lordship of Christ; the task of
conversion is that of the Holy Spirit.

The West African scene offers some specific opportunities
for building missiological bridges to Muslims through dialogue. The religious brotherhoods, which were previously
discussed, present some concrete options and possibilities for
Muslims and Christians to enter into dialogue and together
participate in and share God's blessing. This is especially
true of more orthodox, learned Muslims. The dynamic power
of blessing can become an effective stepping stone to further
sharing.

The *tariqa* communities present a viable opportunity for
dialogue through blessing because the concept of *baraka* is

viewed as a source of spiritual power by these Muslims. The
communal, sacramental, theological, and sociological dynamics
of the brotherhoods indicate that their *zawiya* centers and
communities can become a place where Muslim and Christian
leaders can meet and grow in appreciation of one another.
The fact that the Christian comes with the *baraka* of God
deepens and strengthens the potential for profitable encounter, communication, and witness.

David W. Shenk (1977) reports of a continuing dialogical
interaction in which he and others have been participating
in a suburb of Nairobi, Kenya for several years. His in-
tuition is that Muslims and Christians would do well to seriously attempt to meet one another in dialogue and inter-
community relationship. He and other missionaries have set
up a Christian community across the street from a Sufi brotherhood *zawiya*. His convictions are "that the ramifications
of any such particular encounter would likely be mutually en-
riching both in the microcosmic setting as well as within the
macrocosmic arena of general Christian-Muslim dialogue, witness, and understanding" (Shenk, 1977:i).

Shenk suggests that the concept of blessing in the book of
Hebrews is an excellent beginning point for fruitful dialogue. Hebrews is especially relevant for dialogue with Sufi
brotherhood members because it is community-oriented and relates well to the spiritual and theological aspirations of
Sufism. If the Christian Church can somehow reflect a wor-
shipping lifestyle and theology based on the covenant of
blessing found in Hebrews, the Gospel will become more attractive to Muslims and will be affirmed and appreciated by them.

In enthusiasm for such dialogue, Christians must be careful to avoid syncretism. While syncretistic developments
point out commonalities of the two faiths, syncretism, in the
end, will destroy dialogical enrichment and lead to a demise
of one's faith. "Syncretism is not creative, it represents
an erosion of the faith contribution which a community has to
offer. Syncretism impoverishes respective heritages; dialogue enriches" (Shenk, 1977:22).

While Shenk speaks out of an East African setting, his
insights and suggestions are readily adaptable to West Africa.
In West Africa the Sufi brotherhoods are partiuclarly strong
in the urban centers. The Church should seriously consider
establishing Christian communities near these centers for the
purpose of dialogue and witness. This can be an effective way
for the dynamic power of blessing to become a missiological
bridge to Islam in West Africa.

BLESSING AS A LITURGICAL BRIDGE TO ISLAM

Another significant link in the bridge to Islam is that of blessing within the rituals of the Church. Africans in general, and Muslims in particular, see ritual as a basic element of religious expression. It is often through ritual that West Africans comprehend the truth of their faith. Ritual becomes a link to the spiritual world.

Ritual is also a basic element of the western Church. While there are some churches that make more elaborate use of rituals than others, all Christian Churches see ritual as a mode of communicating and grasping the message of their faith. Western ritual is quite different from that in Islamic West Africa, but it is ritual and serves a similar purpose.

For the Christian Church to have a continuing and growing impact on West Africa, it must recreate the required association and relationship between theology and ritual. The Gospel dare not be reduced to an ideology, but, instead, must be dramatized in living rituals which communicate the deep spiritual meaning and power of God's salvation.

A strong emphasis on the impact of blessing within the liturgical realm of the Church can help it reintegrate and reinterpret the Gospel in ways that will attract Muslims to its message. This will require developing rituals of blessing that fit the African world view, that are compatible to and expressive of the deep needs and hopes of these cherished people of God. This process will not be easy. The solidification of western rituals, which has sometimes led to the "arrest and sterility of the African religious genius" (Trimingham, 1955:36), will have to be uprooted and remolded so they can become legitimate African Christian rituals and expressions of prayer and faith. Blessing will then become incarnated and communicated in African symbols, songs, poetry, and dance. Only in this way will the Gospel of blessing avoid the semblance of alienism and be able to sink its roots deep into the African soil.

It is crucial that the Christian Church recognize the importance and validity of communicating the blessing of God through rituals. Rituals are liturgical expressions of divine and human interrelationships. As such, they are pertinent because relationships are focal points of existence for Africans. Rituals dare not be impersonal and abstract. They must communicate life.

Because a life of blessing is highly valued by West African Muslims, a life of *baraka* encompassing both material and spiritual blessings, relevant rituals of the Church will be needed to communicate effectively the Good News. In rituals, West African Muslims can understand how God deals with his people; how he blesses them with grace, forgiveness, and power.

In our examination of rituals as links to West African Muslims, we shall include rituals that are basic to worship and the rites of passage. The blessing of God can be communicated through greetings, prayers and praises, the ministry of the word, and benedictions. Sacramental rituals are also potent forms of communicating blessing. Other rites of blessing also need to be incorporated into the liturgical life of the Church; rites that bring the blessing of God to individuals and families at crucial points of transition and crisis.

Blessing in the Environment of Worship

Worship is a central part of the Islamic faith and life. Prayer, in particular, is a required pillar of faith to which all true Muslims are obedient. However, because of their distrust of the Christian Church, most Muslims refuse to enter a church building. Yet, many curious and inquisitive Muslims will come near a congregation at worship if they hear worship forms that are intriguing and familiar. In northern Cameroon several Muslims sat outside a Christian congregation at worship when new indigenous worship forms began to be used by that particular church.

Where Muslims are in the minority, the Christian Church may consider retaining its basic worship patterns within the sanctuary. However, its prayers and praises, greetings and benedictions, its ministry of the word, must be done in such a way that it attracts Muslim listeners and communicates blessing. In other words, the forms these rituals and spiritual exercises take must fit the African image of worship. God and his blessing must become personal and alive.

Within a predominantly Muslim context, the Christian Church must consider the possibility of changing the environment of its worship of God from a conventional western setting to one more attractive and in tune with Muslims. It may be more conducive to use some Islamic forms of worship through which the blessing and Gospel of God in Christ can be communicated. This will require creative ingenuity, bold courage, and a sensitive understanding of West African Islam. But the hope of achieving an effective witness to Muslims demands a thorough consideration and possible reorientation.

This hope is not devoid of problems. A potential problem in the use of Islamic worship forms concerns where the Muslim convert places his allegiance. Within Islam, the *shari'a* (law) is the core of faith and practice to which the obedience of adherents is directed and demanded. When Christ replaces the law as the center of faith, will the use of Islamic forms help the Muslim convert grow in his allegiance to Christ, or will they detract from Christ and cause the new believer to think that the Christian faith is nothing more than allegiance to forms and laws? However, the danger that the latter may become the case in some instances should not prevent the Church from considering the use of several Islamic forms of worship in a Christian context.

Kastner (1978) is aware of the need for a new approach in worship for the Church in an Islamic environment. In discussing the Church's witness to nomadic Muslim Fulanis and encouraging Christians to witness to them, she writes:

We should help them begin to worship in their camp. Here they can prepare things as they are used to, under a tree, and at a time that is best for them. It will be difficult for them to come to the church at the usual times. By Fulani Christians having their own worship, the nonbelieving Fulani people will begin to see the value of the Christian faith, and, also, they will not look on it as a strange thing. Those who are around them will come close (p. 5).

The strategy of Kastner is evident in the concluding chapter of her book. Entitled "How to Begin a Fulani Church," the chapter is significant in that it breaks away from the traditional mission approach which insists that Muslim converts join the existing Christian Church and shed their own customs, culture, and possibly their own language.

A church composed of Fulani converts is desirable at this time. People of a cultural group relate best to each other. When non-Christian Fulani see them, they will be attracted to Jesus Christ as being theirs and not think of Him as another culture. Christian Fulani will attract non-Christian Fulani to their gatherings and times of sharing. They can set their own times for worship and study, appoint their leaders and sing their kind of song. They can meet where it is convenient and develop their own style of worship, teaching, and exhortation, all within the Fulani cultural framework (p. 49).

Blessing in the Sacraments of the Church

The impact of blessing in the environment of worship will
be enriched and deepened if, correspondingly, the sacraments
of the Church become channels of blessing. Both baptism and
Holy Communion are means of grace and blessing. They can
become a bridge in the Church's ministry and mission to Muslims.

At the same time, however, we must recognize the fact that
baptism, in particular, is often viewed negatively by Muslims.
It is seen by them as an act indicating separation from their
Islamic community and the total rejection of Islam itself.
This negative image may be reduced if Muslims begin to understand that in the Christian sacrament of baptism God is bestowing his blessing. The negative image could be further
reduced if baptism became more and more a communal act and
experience.

Baptism. As the rite of incorporation and initiation,
baptism conveys the grace and blessing of God. It ushers the
baptised person into the Kingdom of God and makes him a viable
and hopefully responsible member of the Church. Through baptism the believer has the dynamic potential of living a life
of faith and obedience.

Within the West African context, it seems appropriate that
baptism be closely related to, if not entirely integrated
with, the act and ritual of name giving. This is applicable
to those Christian faiths that baptise children. In baptism
the person becomes a child of God; he receives a new name, a
Christian name. This name is indicative of his new relationship with God.

Among Muslims in West Africa, the child should probably be
baptised eight days after birth to correspond to the normal
name giving ceremony. Because the home and family are central to these Africans, it may be best if the congregation
come to the home of the person to be baptised and participate
in the festive celebration of this pivotal event. Hopefully,
the pastor has already spent time with the family of the
newborn child and has prayed for the child and the family.
In these ways the sacrament of baptism becomes enmeshed in the
fabric of community without losing its precise meaning and impact.

For those Christian faiths that practice adult baptism
only, they can consider dedicating the child on the eighth

day after his birth or possibly relate the celebration of
baptism to circumcision. While circumcision often carries
with it the connotation of becoming Muslim in many African
communities--which may become a difficult barrier-- the
Church may still use this puberty rite as an appropriate moment for incorporating converts into the Church. The catechetical instruction required can be an appropriate part of
the instruction given the novitiate who awaits the moment
when he becomes an adult. Those Christian faiths that baptise children should consider incorporating confirmation or
affirmation of baptism into the rite of circumcision. The
communal aspect of confirmation fits well the communal nature
of circumcision.

An additional factor in baptism to be considered is that
it be viewed as a communal rite of blessing, not just an individual one. The impact of community is so powerful in West
African society that the Church dare not insist on individual
conversions and baptisms. The approach must be a community-
oriented one. Jørgensen (1979) reports that the Lutheran
World Federation and cooperating churches and missions are
deeply conscious of this fact in their strategy for mission
to the Fulani people.

> Thus the best approach will be along the natural lines of
> relationship within the various social units. The same
> was stressed by the recent Consultation of Lutheran
> Churches on Work in West Africa: Taking into considera-
> tion the strong commitment of the Fulani to his community
> and religion, the proclamation of the Gospel to the al-
> ready existing communities and social units should be en-
> couraged.... (p. 300).

The Lord's Supper. Like baptism, the Lord's Supper is
also a rite of blessing and a means of grace. Because it in-
herently involves community, it usually avoids the tendency
to individualize the Christian faith. Yet, the Church must
consistently be conscious of that possibility among believers.

African forms should be used to communicate the biblical
meaning of the life-giving blessing in this sacrament. For
example, for many West Africans, millet is the staple food.
If they have not eaten millet porridge, they feel they have
not eaten at all. Because of this, the Church should consider using this element in the sacrament of Holy Communion.
This is because it communicates the fact that Christ who is
the "Bread of Life," without whom there is no life, no meaning
to life, comes to them and blesses them.

An important aspect of the sacrament to emphasize is its
holiness. In the Eucharist God comes to the Christian and
his community and is very near. God's *baraka* gives the believers renewed power, strength, and forgiveness. An aura of
respect for the holiness of this encounter between God and
man will communicate to Muslims the deep awareness of God
that Christians have, and that they intimately experience
the presence of God. This will relate to Muslims that God
is real and alive in the Christian faith. The holiness of
baraka is a vital part of their awareness of and belief in
God. To see that holiness is not only a Muslim virtue prevalent in holy men and saints, but also a Christian virtue,
will enhance their openness to the Gospel.

Therefore, the Lord's Supper must become a holy moment
in the life of the Church. As the believers exhibit in
African emotions, gestures, and expressions their total
awareness of the presence, power, and blessing of God in the
sacrament, the interest and receptivity of their Muslim
friends will increase.

Not only must respect for God's holiness be present in the
sacraments and the worship setting, but the place of worship
must also be guarded and preserved as a holy place. In this
way God's blessing is present. If the Christian Church does
not care properly for the house of worship, its neglect will
destroy its witness to Muslims. The author remembers with
disgust a time when cows entered a Christian Church and slept
there. The resulting ridicule of the Christian Church by
Muslims was unbearable to hear. The Christian Church, if it
is to be an effective witness to Muslims in West Africa, must
be careful to see that its sanctuaries are holy places of
worship where God can encounter people and bestow on them
his blessings.

Blessing in Other Rites of the Church

In addition to the sacraments and the rite of circumcision,
the Church has potential for witnessing to Muslims through
incorporating blessing in other significant rites. Two
such moments when the Church can become a channel of blessing
and communicate God's love, presence, and power are marriage
and funerals.

Marriage. For many Muslims, a wedding ceremony is one
ritual where *baraka* is present. The bride and groom in many
Muslim societies are viewed as being charged with *baraka*.
The Muslim cleric plays a strategic role in the ceremony.

The wedding is an opportunity for a Christian pastor to witness to the blessing of God. Unfortunately, the West African Church has often become a participant in western administrative procedures. This often means that all recognized marriages are civil marriages. In many rural areas this results in traditional tribal marriages not being recognized by the government. This, in turn, has led the Church to refuse to bless such marriages.

Muslim clerics, on the other hand, seem not to be bound by these administrative procedures. This means that their impact on society, and the blessing of God they bring, is a significant force and is highly valued by the people.

The Christian Church needs to re-evaluate its position on blessing marriages. There would be a more positive view of the Church and the Christian faith if the pastor were totally involved in the three aspects of the marriage: arranging for the marriage, the marrying, and the blessing of the bride and groom.

In the marriage rite the blessing of God can become a binding force that helps make the marriage a more secure and lasting relationship. If the Church were thoroughly involved in the marriage process, its effect would be a more positive and attractive witness to Muslim society.

Funeral. When death occurs in a family, the Church has a strategic opportunity for witness and for bestowing the blessing of God. While the funeral customs vary from area to area, the Christian pastor serving in an Islamic region needs to be viewed as a man of blessing who is involved in the total death and mourning process.

The exact rituals a Christian pastor may perform or be a part of will vary. His actions depend on whether he is working among an animistic-becoming-Christian tribe whose neighbors are Muslims, or whether he is serving in a predominantly Muslim community where there is a small Christian community developing. In his and the Church's concern for reaching out to Muslims with the Gospel, he should make every effort possible to function in such ways during the death process so as to enhance their receptivity of his ministry without compromising or syncretizing Christian beliefs.

If there is a ritual washing of the deceased's body, the minister can contribute to the holiness and sanctity of the process through participation in the washing and in the

leading of the prayers. Thought must be given as to the
meaning of the washing, but its tie with Islamic practice
need not deter one from being involved in this event.

Proper and speedy care of the deceased body will indicate
to Muslims the cherished concern of the Church for the dead
and those who mourn. At the funeral and burial, the pastor
has an opportunity to bring a message of salvation and hope.
His prayers of blessing are particularly significant at this
moment.

During the mourning period, which is often 40 days for
Muslims, the clergyman is involved as the blesser of the
food prepared and the people gathered. Because Africans
spend a great deal of time with the mourning family, it is
a potentially fruitful time for the pastor to share the
Good News. It will be well received because it is within a
cultural context that is similar to an Islamic one, yet one
which retains a Christian character.

Thus, we see that the Church has numerous opportunities
for bestowing the blessing of God through worship and various
rituals. We have briefly discussed the main rituals. There
are other occasions for the pastor and the Church to bring
the Gospel as a message of blessing. Some important occasions are seasonal prayers for the planting and harvesting
of the crops, prayers for rain, and other specific needs.
These prayers and rituals will indicate to Muslims that God,
through the Christian Church, is concerned that his people
have a life filled with *baraka*. If all these opportunities
are used in a proper manner by the Church in West Africa,
it will enhance its witness to the Muslim community.

Summary

As the Christian Church looks at the millions of Muslims in West Africa, it cannot help but be gripped by the awesome chasm that exists. It is frustrated by the tremendous barriers that prevent these children of Abraham from becoming inheriters of the Kingdom of God through faith in Jesus Christ.

Yet, the Church seems to be stymied in its concern for and outreach to the Muslims of West Africa. Past mistakes, rejection, and hostility are some of the reasons. The Church too often seems satisfied and content with growth only among the non-Muslim population of West Africa.

But the commands of Christ to be his witnesses forces the Church to re-evaluate its position on mission to Muslims. Bridges *can* be built to the Islamic sector of West Africa. Blessing is a strategic concept that must be basic to any bridge--theological, missiological, and liturgical--that the Church attempts to build to Muslims in West Africa.

The implementation of blessing will mean that the Church must reorient its strategy so that it becomes concerned with all aspects of its life and message--priestly, prophetic, diaconal, and missionary. The incorporation of blessing into the ministry, worship, outreach, and theology of the Church in Africa will enhance its witness. Its emphasis will increase the Africans' receptivity to the Gospel because it encompasses the solidarity and totality of God's relationship to man, especially at points of transition and crisis. By blessing, God ministers to the material and spiritual well-being of man. Through blessing God participates in the community through word and ritual. In an Islamic African context, blessing is correctly perceived in powerful, mystical, sacred, and symbolic terms. In this way, it has tremendous potential for the Church in its holistic mission and ministry to the people of God in West Africa.

It is particularly crucial that the Church recognize the strategic centrality of ritual in the life of West Africans. For its witness to be effective, the Church must develop and implement creative, personal and communal rituals that readily communicate the Gospel of blessing. Without proper rituals, the impact of the message of new life in Christ will be, at most, mediocre.

The future of the West African Islamic community is at stake. The dynamic potential of holistic blessing stands ready to help bring this large, growing community into the life-giving sheepfold of the Good Shepherd.

Bibliography

ABUN-NASR, Jamil M.
1965 *The Tijaniyya: A Sufi Order in the Modern World.*
      London: Oxford University Press.

ALI, Abdullah Yusuf
1946 *The Holy Qur'an; Text, Translation, and Commentary,*
      Vols. 1-3. 3rd ed. New York: Hafner Publishing Co.

ARNETT, E. J.
1922 *The Rise of the Sokoto Fulani.* Kano, Nigeria:
      Emirate Printing Department.

BACHMAN, John W.
1976 "Theology and Communication; Towards a Theological
      and Theoretical Context for the Rule of the Church
      in Dealing with Modern Media of Communication,"
      WACC Journal, vol. 23, no. 2:14-18.

BAUER, Johannes B., ed.
1970 *Encyclopaedia of Biblical Theology.* trans. Joseph
      Blenkinsopp, et al. London: Sheed and Ward.

BEATY, James M.
1963 *Early Christian Blessings; A Form and Function Study
      of Formulae Used as Greetings and Blessing in the
      Early Church.* PhD. Dissertation, Nashville: Vander-
      bilt University. Ann Arbor: University of Michigan
      Microfilms.

BECK, Hartmut and BROWN, Colin
  1976   "Peace," *The New International Dictionary of New
         Testament Theology*, vol. 2. ed. Colin Brown. Grand
         Rapids: Zondervan Publishing Company.

BRAND, Eugene
  1973   "New Accents in Baptism and Eucharist," *Worship:
         Good News in Action*, ed. Mandus Egge. Minneapolis:
         Augsburg Publishing House.

BROWN, Colin, ed.
  1975, 1976 *The New International Dictionary of New Testa-
         ment Theology*, vols. 1-2. Grand Rapids: Zondervan
         Publishing Company.

BRUN, Lyder
  1932   *Segen und Fluch im Urchristentum*. Oslo: Jacob Dybwad.

BURKE, O. Michael
  1973   *Among the Dervishes*. London: The Octagon Press Ltd.

BUTTRICK, George A., ed.
  1954   *The Interpreter's Bible*, vol. 9. New York: Abingdon-
         Cokesbury Press.
  1962   *Interpreter's Dictionary of the Bible*, vol. 1. Nash-
         ville: Abingdon Press.

CALVIN, John
  1961   *The Epistles of Paul the Apostle to the Romans and
         the Thessalonians, Calvin's Commentaries*, vol. 8.
         trans. Ross Mackenzie. Grand Rapids: William B.
         Eerdmans Publishing Company.

CHELHOD, Jospeh
  1955   "La Baraka Chez Les Arabes," *Revue de l'Histoire des
         Religions*, 148:68-88.

CHEYNE, T. K. and BLACK, J. Sutherland, eds.
  1899   *Encyclopedia Biblica*, vol. 1. London: Adam and
         Charles Black.

CLARKE, Adam
  n.d.   *The New Testament of our Lord and Saviour Jesus
         Christ, Volume 2, Romans to Revelations*. New York:
         Abingdon-Cokesbury Press.

COOKE, Francis T.
1935 "Ibn al-Qayim's Kitab al-Ruh," *The Moslem World*, 25: 129-44.

CRAGG, Kenneth
1964 *The Dome and the Rock*. London: SPCK.
1973 *The Mind of the Qur'an*. London: George Allen & Unwin Ltd.

CRANFIELD, C. E. B.
1958 "Divine and Human Action: The Biblical Concept of Worship," *Interpretation*, 22:387-98.

CULLY, Kendig B., ed.
1962 *Confirmation: History, Doctrine and Practice*. Greenwich, Conn.: The Seabury Press.

DELLING, Gerhard
1962 *Worship in the New Testament*. Philadelphia: The Westminister Press.

DOLBEER, William H.
1907 *The Benediction*. Philadelphia: Lutheran Publication Society.

DOUGLAS, Elmer H.
1948 "Al-Shadhili; A North African Sufi, According to Ibn al-Sabbagh," *The Muslim World*, 38:257-78.

DOUTTE, Edmond
1909 *Magie et Religion dans l"Afrique du Nord*. Algiers: A. Jourdan.

DRIVER, S. R. et al., eds.
1922 *The International Critical Commentary*, vol. 28. 3rd ed. New York: Scribner's Sons.

DURKHEIM, Emile
1954 *The Elementary Forms of the Religious Life*. trans. Joseph W. Swain. Glencoe, Ill.: The Free Press.

EGGE, Mandus, ed.
1973 *Worship: Good News in Action*. Minneapolis: Augsburg Publishing House.

EICHRODT, Walther
1961, 1967 *Theology of the Old Testament*, vols. 1-2. trans. J. A. Baker. Philadelphia: The Westminister Press.

EICKELMAN, Dale F.
  1976 *Moroccan Islam: Tradition and Society in a Pilgrimage
         Center*. Austin: University of Texas Press.

ELERT, Werner
  1973 *The Lord's Supper Today*. trans. Mertin Bertram.
         St. Louis: Concordia Publishing House.

EVANS-PRITCHARD, E. E.
  1949 *The Sanusi of Cyrenaica*. London: Oxford University
         Press.

FALLDING, Harold
  1974 *The Sociology of Religion*. New York: McGraw-Hill.

FARAH, Caesar, E.
  1968 *Islam; Beliefs and Observances*. Woodbury, N.Y.:
         Barron's Educational Series, Inc.

FRASER, David A.
  1979 "An 'Engel Scale' For Muslim Work," *The Gospel and
         Islam: A 1978 Compendium*, ed. Don M. McCurry.p. 164-77.
         Monrovia, CA: MARC

FROELICH, J. C.
  1962 *Les Musulman d'Afrique Noire*. Paris: Editions de
         l'Orante.

GEERTZ, Clifford
  1968 *Islam Observed; Religious Development in Morocco and
         Indonesia*. New Haven: Yale University Press.

GIBB, Hamilton A.R.
  1962 *Studies on the Civilization of Islam*. London:
         Routledge and Kegan Paul, Ltd.

GIBB, Hamilton A. R. and KRAMER, J. H., eds.
  1965 *The Shorter Encyclopaedia of Islam*. Ithaca, N.Y.:
         Cornell University Press.

GILBERT, W. Kent, ed.
  1969 *Confirmation and Education*. Philadelphia: Fortress
         Press.

GILLILAND, Dean S.
  1971 *African Traditional Religion in Transition*. Unpub-
         lished PhD. Dissertation. Hartford Seminary Foundation.

GLASSER, Arthur F.
   1976 "Is Friendly Dialogue Enough?" *Missiology*, 4:259-66.
   1979 "Power Encounter in Conversion from Islam," *The Gos-
         pel and Islam; A 1978 Compendium*. ed. Don M. McCurry.
         Monrovia, CA: MARC.

GOLDZIHER, Ignaz
   1971 *Muslim Studies*, vol. 2. trans. C.R. Barber and S. M.
         Stern. Chicago: Aldine-Atherton Inc.

GRAY, G. Buchanan
   1899 "Anointing," *Encyclopaedia Biblica*, vol. 1. eds.
         T. K. Cheyne and J. Sutherland Black. London: Adam
         and Charles Black.

GREENBERG, Joseph
   1946 *The Influence of Islam on a Sudanese Religion*.
         Seattle: University of Washington Press.

GROSE, George B.
   1976 *Foundations for Dialogue Between Judaism, Christian-
         ity, and Islam*. PhD. Dissertation, Claremont School
         of Theology. Ann Arbor: University of Michigan
         Microfilms.

GROSS, Heinrich
   1970 "Peace," *Encyclopedia of Biblical Theology*. ed.
         Johannes B. Bauer. trans. Joseph Blenkinsopp et al.
         London: Sheed and Ward.

HARRELSON, W. J.
   1962 "Blessings and Cursings," *Interpreter's Dictionary
         of the Bible*, vol. 1. ed. George A. Buttrick. Nash-
         ville: Abingdon Press.

HERBERT, A. S.
   1962 *Genesis 12-50*. London: SCM Press Ltd.

JEFFERY, Arthur, ed.
   1962 *A Reader on Islam*. The Hague: Mouton & Company.

JOHNSTON, H. A. S.
   1967 *The Fulani Empire of Sokoto*. London: Oxford Univer-
         sity Press.

JØRGENSON, Knud
   1979 *The Role and Function of the Media in the Mission of
         the Church, with Particular Reference to Africa*. Un-
         published PhD. diss. Fuller Theological Seminary.

KASTNER, Elsie
  1978 *Let's Help the Fulani People*, rev. by Gerald Swank.
        Cedar Grove, N.J.: Sudan Interior Mission.

KRAEMER, Hendrik
  1962 *Why Christianity of All Religions?* Philadelphia:
        The Westminister Press.

KRAFT, Charles H.
  1973 "The Incarnation, Cross-Cultural Communication, and
        Communication Theory," *Evangelical Missions Quarterly*,
        9:277-84
  1974 "Guidelines for Developing a Message Geared to the
        Horizon of Receptivity, parts 1-2," *Media in Islamic
        Culture*. ed. C. Richard Shumaker. Marseille, France:
        International Christian Broadcasters and Evangelical
        Literature Overseas, p. 17-33.
  1979 *Christianity in Culture: A Study in Dynamic Biblical
        Theologizing in Cross-Cultural Perspective*. Maryknoll,
        N.Y.: Orbis Books.

KRITZECK, James and LEWIS, William H., eds.
  1969 *Islam in Africa*. New York: Van Norstrand-Reinhold
        Company.

LADD, George E.
  1959 *The Gospel of the Kingdom*. Grand Rapids: William B.
        Eerdmans Publishing Company.

LEENHARDT, F. J.
  1955 "La Signification de la notion de parole dans la
        Pensée Chrétienne," *Revue d'Histoire et de Philo-
        sophie Religiueses*, 35:263-73.

LENSKI, R. C. H.
  1946a *The Interpretation of St. Mark's Gospel*. Columbus:
         The Wartburg Press.
  1946b *Interpretation of St. Paul's Epistles to the Colos-
         sians, to the Thessalonians, to Timothy, to Titus,
         and to Philemon*. Columbus: The Wartburg Press.

LE TOURNEAU, Roger
  1955 "North Africa: Rigorism and Bewilderment," *Unity
        and Variety in Muslim Civilization*. ed. Gustave E.
        Von Grunebaum. Chicago: University of Chicago Press.

LEVY, Reubin
  1957 *The Social Structures of Islam*. London: Oxford Uni-
        versity Press.

LEWIS, I. M.
  1966 "Introduction," *Islam in Tropical Africa.* ed. I. M.
       Lewis. London: Oxford University Press.

LEWIS, I. M. ed.
  1962 *Islam in Tropical Africa.* London: Oxford University
       Press.

LINGS, Martin
  1971 *A Sufi Saint of the Twentieth Century,* 2nd edition.
       Berkeley: University of California Press.

LUTHER, Martin
  1964 *Luther's Werke, Kritische Gesamtausgabe, (Weimar
       Ausgabe),* vol. 30-32. Reprinted from 1909 edition.
       Weimar: Hermann Böhlaus Nachfolger.

MACDONALD, Duncan B.
  1903 *Development of Muslim Theology, Jurisprudence, and
       Constitutional Theory.* New York: Scribner's.

MACGREGOR, G. H. C.
  1954 "Acts and Romans," *The Interpreter's Bible,* vol. 9.
       ed. George A. Buttrick. New York: Abindgon-Cokes-
       bury Press.

MARGOLIOUTH, D. S.
  1965 "Shadhiliya," *The Shorter Encyclopaedia of Islam.*
       eds. H. A. R. Gibb and J. H. Kramers. Ithaca, N.Y.:
       Cornell University Press.

MARTENSON, Robert R.
  1977 *The Life and Work of Usmaanu bii Fooduye.* Unpublished
       Phd. Dissertation. Hartford Seminary Foundation.

MARTIN, Bratford G.
  1976 *Muslim Brotherhoods in Nineteenth Century Africa.*
       London: Cambridge University Press.

MARTIN, Ralph B.
  1964 *Worship in the Early Church.* Grand Rapids: William
       B. Eerdmans Publishing Company.

MCCURRY, Don M., ed.
  1979 *The Gospel and Islam: A 1978 Compendium.* Monrovia,
       CA: MARC.

MILLER, Patrick D., Jr.
  1975 "Blessing of God: An Interpretation of Numbers 6:
        22-27," *Interpretation*, 29:240-51.

MILTON, John
  1961 *God's Covenant of Blessing*. Rock Island, Ill.;
        Augustana Press.

MOWINCKEL, Sigmund
  1962 *The Psalms in Israel's Worship*. vols. 1-2. Nashville:
        Abingdon Press.

MOWVLEY, H.
  1965 "The Concept and Content of 'Blessing' in the Old
        Testament," *The Bible Translator*, 16:74-80.

MULDER, D. C.
  1977 "Forward," *Christians Meeting Muslims: WCC Papers
        on Ten Years of Christian-Muslim Dialogue*. Geneva:
        World Council of Churches.

MULLER, D.
  1975 "Anoint-*chrio*," *The New International Dictionary of
        New Testament Theology*. vol. 1. ed. Colin Brown.
        Grand Rapids: Zondervan Publishing House.

MÜLLER, F. Max, ed.
  1900 *The Sacred Books of the East*. vol. 9. Oxford: The
        Clarendon Press.

MURRAY, John
  1968 *The Epistle to the Romans*. Grand Rapids: William B.
        Eerdmans Publishing Company.

MURTONEN, A.
  1959 'The Use and Meaning of the Words '*lebarek*' and '*ber-
        akah*' in the Old Testament," *Vetus Testamentum*, 9:
        158-77.

MUSK, Bill
  1979 "Popular Islam: The Hunger of the Heart," *The Gospel
        and Islam: A 1978 Compendium*. Monrovia, CA: MARC.

NACPIL, Emerito
  1968-69 "Between Promise and Fulfillment," *South East
        Asia Journal of Theology*, 10:166-81.

NASR, Seyyed Hossein
  1966 *Ideals and Realities of Islam*. London: George Allen
      and Unwin Ltd.
  1972 *Sufi Essays*. Albany, N.Y.: State University of New
      York Press.

NEILL, Stephen
  1964 *A History of Christian Missions*. Baltimore: Penguin
      Books, Inc.

NICHOLSON, Reynold A.
  1921 *Studies in Islamic Mysticism*. London: Cambridge
      University Press.

OTTO, Rudolf
  1950 *The Idea of the Holy*. 2nd ed. trans. J. W. Harvey.
      London: Oxford University Press.

PADEN, John N.
  1973 *Religion and Political Culture in Kano*. Berkeley:
      University of California Press.

PADWICK, Constance E.
  1961 *Muslim Devotions: A Study of Prayer Manuals in
      Common Use*. London: SPCK.

PALMER, E. H.
  1900 "The Qur'an," part 2. *The Sacred Books of the East*.
      vol. 9. ed. F. Max Müller. Oxford: The Clarendon
      Press.

PALMER, Paul F.
  1958 "The Purpose of Anointing the Sick: A Reappraisal,"
      Theological Studies, 19/3:309-44.

PARRATT, J. K.
  1969 "The Laying on of Hands in the New Testament,"
      Expository Times, 80:210-14.

PARRINDER, E. Geoffrey
  1973 *A Dictionary of Non-Christian Religions*. Philadel-
      phia: The Westminister Press.

PEDERSEN, Johannes
  1926, 1940 *Israel: Its Life and Culture*. vols. 1-4.
      London: Geoffrey Cumberlege; Oxford University Press.

PEERBHAI, Adam
  1974 *Complete Primary Madressa Text*. Durban, South Africa:
       Universal Printing Works.

PELIKAN, Jaroslav
  1958 *Luther's Works*. vol. 14. St. Louis: Concordia
       Publishing House.

PICKTHALL, Mohammed M.
  1953 *The Meaning of the Glorious Koran*. New York: The
       New American Library of World Literature, Inc.

PLUMMER, Alfred
  1922 *A Critical and Exegetical Commentary on the Gospel
       According to St. Luke, The International Critical
       Commentary*. vol. 28, 3rd. ed. eds. S. R. Driver
       et al. New York: Scribner's Sons.

ROBSON, James
  1936 "Blessings on the Prophet," *The Moslem World*, 26:
       365-71.

RODINSON, Maxime
  1971 *Mohammed*. trans. Anne Carter. New York: Pantheon
       Books.

ROWLEY, Harold H.
  1950 "The Meaning of Sacrifice in the Old Testament,"
       Bulletin of the John Rylands Library, 33/1:74-110.

SCHARBERT, Josef
  1958 *Solidarität in Segen und Fluch im Alten Testament
       und in seiner Welt. I. Vaterfluch und Vatersegen*.
       Bonn: Hanstein.

SCHENK, Wolfgang
  1967 *Der Segen im Neuen Testament*. Berlin: Evangelische
       Verlagansalt.

Schimmel, Annemarie
  1975 *Mystical Dimensions of Islam*. Chapel Hill, N. C.:
       University of North Carolina Press.

SCHUON, Frithjof
  1969 *Dimensions of Islam*. trans. P. N. Townsend. London:
       George Allen and Unwin Ltd.

SHENK, David W.
1977 *The Tariqa: A Meeting Place for Christians and Muslims*. Unpublished manuscript.

SHUMAKER, C. Richard, ed.
1974 *Media in Islamic Culture*. Marseilles: International Christian Broadcasters and Evangelical Literature Overseas.

SMITH, Margaret
1976 *The Way of the Mystics*. London: Sheldon Press.

STENNES, Leslie H.
1978 Personal letter.

STENNING, Derrick J.
1959 *Savannah Nomads*. London: Oxford University Press.

TABATABA'I, Norbert
1969 "Evolving Social Patterns," *Islam in Africa*. eds. James Kritzeck and William H. Lewis. New York: Van Norstrand-Reinhold Company.

TRIMINGHAM, J. Spencer
1955 *The Christian Church and Islam in West Africa*. London: SCM Press.
1959 *Islam in West Africa*. Oxford: The Clarendon Press.
1968 *The Influence of Islam upon Africa*. London: Longmans, Green and Co., Ltd.
1971 *The Sufi Orders in Islam*. Oxford: The Clarendon Press.

TURNER, Bryan S.
1974 *Weber and Islam: A Critical Study*. London: Routledge and Kegan Paul.

VAN DEN DOEL, Anthonie
1968 *Blessing and Cursing in the New Testament and Related Literature*. Phd. Dissertation. Northwestern University. Ann Arbor: University of Michigan Microfilms.

VAWTER, Bruce
1977 *On Genesis: A New Reading*. Garden City, N.Y.: Doubleday And Company, Inc.

VON GRUNEBAUM, Gustave E.
1953 *Medieval Islam: A Study in Cultural Orientation*. 2nd ed. Chicago: University of Chicago Press.

VON GRUNEBAUM, Gustave E. ed.
   1955 *Unity and Variety in Muslim Civilization*. Chicago:
         University of Chicago Press.

VON RAD, Gerhard
   1972 *Genesis*. London: SCM Press.

WALLACE, Anthony F.C.
   1956 "Revitalization Movements," *American Anthropologist*,
         58: 264-81.

WALLACE, W.
   1896 "Notes on a Journey Through the Sokoto Empire and
         Bornu in 1894," *Geographical Journal*, 8: 210-21.

WEBER, Max
   1947 *The Theory of Social and Economic Organization*. trans.
         A.M. Henderson. New York: Oxford University Press.

WEISER, Artur
   1962 *The Psalms*. Philadelphia: The Westminister Press.

WEST, Edward N.
   1962 "The Rites of Christian Initiation in the Early
         Church," *Confirmation: History, Doctrine, and
         Practice*. ed. Kendig B. Cully. Greenwich, Conn.:
         The Seabury Press.

WESTERMANN, Claus
   1978 *Blessing in the Bible and the Life of the Church*.
         trans. Keith Crim. Philadelphia: Fortress Press.

WESTERMARCK, Edvard
   1926 *Ritual and Belief in Morocco*. vol. 1. London: Mac-
         milland Co., Ltd.

WILKEN, Robert L.
   1972 "The Christianizing of Abraham: The Interpretation of
         Abraham in Early Christianity," *Concordia Theological
         Monthly*, 43: 723-31.

ZIADEH, Nicola A.
   1958 *Sanusiya: A Study of a Revitalist Movement in Islam*.
         Leiden: E. J. Brill

ZWEMER, Samuel M.
   1939 *Studies in Popular Islam*. London: The Sheldon Press.

Biblical
and Quranic Index

All biblical quotes are from the *Revised Standard Version*.

All Quranic quotes are from Pickthall's *The Meaning of the Glorious Koran*.

General Index

About the Author

Dr. Larry Lenning is pastor of Bethlehem Lutheran Church, Granada Hills, California. From 1968 to 1975 he served as a missionary to the Evangelical Lutheran Church of Cameroon, working as district pastor, Bible School teacher, and extension seminary professor. From 1975 to 1978 he served as pastor of Our Saviour's Lutheran Church, Audubon, Iowa.

Pastor Lenning is a graduate of Waldorf and Wartburg Colleges and Luther Theological Seminary. He has done graduate work at the University of Washington and Fuller Theological Seminary. In addition, he has studied French at Acceuil Fraternel and Alliance Francaise in France.

Larry Lenning is a native of Lake Mills, Iowa, and is married to Leota Gebers of Auburn, Nebraska. They are the parents of three children.

BOOKS BY THE
WILLIAM CAREY LIBRARY

GENERAL

Challenge and Crisis in Missionary Medicine by David J. Seel,
1979, 160 pp.

Christ and Caesar in Christian Missions by Wade Coggins and
E.L. Frizen, Jr., 1979, 160 pp.

Church Growth and Christian Mission by Donald A. McGavran,
1965, 256 pp.

Church Growth and Group Conversion by Donald McGavran,
J.W. Pickett, A.L. Warnshuis, & G.H. Singh, 1973, 128 pp.

Committed Communities: Fresh Streams for World Missions by
Charles J. Mellis, 1976, 160 pp.

Crucial Dimensions in World Evangelization by Arthur F.
Glasser, et al., 1976, 512 pp.

Everything You Need to Grow a Messianic Synagogue by Phillip
E. Goble, 1974, 176 pp.

God's Way to Keep a Church Going and Growing by Vergil
Gerber, 1973, 96 pp.

The Indigenous Church and the Missionary by Melvin Hodges,
1978, 108 pp.

STRATEGY OF MISSION

*Education of Missionaries' Children: The Neglected Dimension
of World Mission* by Bruce Lockerbie, 1975, 76 pp.

An Evangelical Agenda: 1984 and Beyond by the Billy Graham
Center, 1979, 234 pp.

Evangelicals Face the Future by Donald E. Hoke, 1978, 184 pp.

Manual for Accepted Missionary Candidates by Marjorie Collins,
1978, 144 pp.

Manual for Missionaries on Furlough by Marjorie Collins, 1972,
160 pp.

The Ministry of Development in Evangelical Perspective by
Robert L. Hancock, 1979, 128 pp.

A Manual for Church Growth Surveys by Ebbie C. Smith, 1976,
144 pp.

*Mission: A Practical Approach to Church-Sponsored Mission
Work* by Daniel C. Hardin, 1978, 264 pp.

Mission-Church Dynamics: An African Experience by Harold
Fuller, 1980, 260 pp.

*Mission Theology: 1948-1975, Years of Worldwide Creative
Tension* by Rodger C. Bassham, 1979, 456 pp.

Readings in Dynamic Indigeneity by Charles Kraft and Tom
Wisley, 1979, 584 pp.

THEOLOGY OF MISSION

Christopaganism or Indigenous Christianity? by Tetsunao
Yamamori & Charles R. Taber, 1974, 242 pp.

*The Conciliar-Evangelical Debate: The Crucial Documents,
1964-1976* by Donald A. McGavran, 1972, 254 pp.

*The Radical Nature of Christianity: Church Growth Eyes Look
at the Supernatural Mission of the Christian and the Church*
by Waldo J. Werning, 1975, 224 pp.

*Social Action vs. Evangelism: An Essay on the Contemporary
Crisis* by William J. Richardson, 1977, 65 pp.

APPLIED ANTHROPOLOGY

Becoming Bilingual: A Guide to Language Learning by Donald
Larson & William Smalley, 1972, 426 pp.

*The Church and Cultures: Applied Anthropology for the
Religious Worker* by Louis J. Luzbetak, 1970, 448 pp.

Communicating the Gospel God's Way by Charles H. Kraft,
1980, 64 pp.

Customs and Cultures: Anthropology for Christian Missions
by Eugene Nida, 1954, 322 pp.

*Gospel and Culture: The Papers of a Consultation on the Gos-
pel and Culture, Convened by the Lausanne Committee*
by John Stott & Robert Coote, 1979, 478 pp.

Manual of Articulatory Phonetics by William A. Smalley, 1973,
522 pp.

Message and Mission: The Communication of the Christian Faith
by Eugene Nida, 1960, 254 pp.

*A People Reborn: Caring Communities, Their Birth and Devel-
opment* by Christian Keysser, 1980, 310 pp.

Readings in Missionary Anthropology II by William A. Smalley,
1978, 912 pp.

*Religion Across Cultures: A Study in the Communication of the
Christian Faith* by Eugene Nida, 1968, 128 pp.

Tips on Taping: Language Recording in the Social Sciences by
Wayne & Lonna Dickerson, 1977, 208 pp.

THEOLOGICAL EDUCATION BY EXTENSION

*The Extension Movement in Theological Education by Extension:
A Call to the Renewal oj the Ministry* by F. Ross Kinsler,
1978, 304 pp.

Here's How: Health Education by Extension Ronald & Edith
Seaton, 1976, 144 pp.

Writing for Theological Education by Extension by Lois McKin-
ney, 1975, 64 pp.

AREA AND CASE STUDIES

Aspects of Pacific Ethnohistory by Alan R. Tippett, 1973,
    216 pp.

Blessing in Mosque and Mission by Larry Lenning, 1980, 272 pp.

A Christian Approach to Muslims: Reflections from West Africa
    by James P. Dretke, 1979, 288 pp.

*Christian Mission to Muslims - The Record: Anglican and Re-
    formed Approaches in India and the Near East, 1800-1938*
    by Lyle L. Vander Werff, 1977, 384 pp.

A Century of Growth: The Katchin Baptist Church of Burma
    by Herman Tegenfeldt, 1974, 540 pp.

Church Growth in Burundi by Donald Hohensee, 1977, 160 pp.

Church Growth in Japan by Tetsunao Yamamori, 1974, 184 pp.

The Church in Africa, 1977 by Charles R. Taber, 1978, 224 pp.

Church Planting in Uganda by Gailyn Van Rhennen, 1976,
    160 pp.

Circle of Harmony: A Case Study in Popular Japanese Buddhism
    by Kenneth J. Dale, 1975, 238 pp.

Ethnic Realities and the Church: Lessons from India by Donald
    A. McGavran, 1979, 272 pp.

Growth and Decline in the Episcopal Church by Wayne B.
    Williamson, 1979, 192 pp.

The Growth of Japanese Churches in Brazil by John Mizuki,
    1978, 240 pp.

*The Growth Crisis in the American Church: A Presbyterian
    Case Study* by Foster H. Shannon, 1977, 176 pp.

*The How and Why of Third World Missions: An Asian Case
    Study* by Marlin L. Nelson, 1976, 256 pp.

Indonesian Revival: Why Two Million Came to Christ by Avery
    T. Willis, Jr., 1977, 288 pp.

*I Will Build My Church: Ten Case Studies of Church Growth in
    Taiwan* by Allen J. Swanson, 1974, 177 pp.

The Navajos are Coming to Jesus by Thomas Dologhan and
    David Scates, 1978, 192 pp.

People Movements in the Punjab by Frederick and Margaret
    Stock, 1975, 388 pp.

Principios Del Crecimiento de la Iglesia by Wayne Weld and
    Donald McGavran, 1970, 446 pp.

The Protestant Movement in Bolivia by C. Peter Wagner, 1970,
    264 pp.

Protestantism in Changing Taiwan: A Call to Creative Response
    by Dorothy A. Raber, 1978, 372 pp.

Protestantism in Latin America: A Bibliographical Guide by
    John H. Sinclair, 1976, 422 pp.

The Religious Dimension in Hispanic Los Angeles by Clifton L.
    Holland, 1974, 550 pp.

The Role of the Faith Mission: A Brazilian Case Study by
    Fred Edwards, 1971, 176 pp.

REFERENCE

An American Directory of Schools and Colleges Offering Missionary Courses by Glen Schwartz, 1973, 266 pp.
Church Growth Bulletin, Second Consolidated Volume (Sept. 1969 - July 1975), by Donald A. McGavran, 1977, 512 pp.
Evangelical Missions Quarterly, Vols. 7-9, 1974, 830 pp.
Evangelical Missions Quarterly, Vols. 10-12, 1978, 960 pp.
Evangelical Missions Quarterly, Vols. 13-15, 1980, 816 pp.
The Means of World Evangelization: Missiological Education at the Fuller School of World Mission by Alvin Martin, 1974, 544 pp.
Word Study Concordance and New Testament (2 Vol. Set) by Ralph & Roberta Winter, 1978, 2-Vol Set.
The World Directory of Mission-Related Educational Institutions by Ted Ward & Raymond Buker, Sr., 1972, 906 pp.

BOOKLETS

The Grounds for a New Thrust in World Mission by Ralph D. Winter, 1977, 32 pp.
The New Macedonia: A Revolutionary New Era in Missions Begins (Lausanne Paper & Address) by Ralph D. Winter, 1975, 32 pp.
Penetrating the Last Frontiers by Ralph D. Winter, 1978, 32 pp.
Protestant Mission Societies by Ralph D. Winter, 1979, 44 pp.
Seeing the Task Graphically by Ralph D. Winter, 1974, 16 pp.
The Six Essential Components of World Evangelization by Ralph D. Winter, 1979, 24 pp.
The Two Structures of God's Redemptive Mission by Ralph D. Winter, 1974, 16 pp.
The World Christian Movement: 1950-1975 by Ralph D. Winter, 1975, 32 pp.

HOW TO ORDER

Send orders to William Carey Library, P.O. Box 128-C, Pasadena, California 91104 (USA). Please allow four to six weeks for delivery in the United States.